NATO Enlargement:
Opinions and Options

Edited by
Jeffrey Simon

1995

National Defense University
Fort McNair
Washington, DC

National Defense University Press Publications

To increase general knowledge and inform discussion, the Institute for National Strategic Studies, through its publication arm the NDU Press, publishes McNair Papers; proceedings of University- and Institute-sponsored symposia; books relating to U.S. national security, especially to issues of joint, combined, or coalition warfare, peacekeeping operations, and national strategy; and a variety of briefer works designed to circulate contemporary comment and offer alternatives to current policy. The Press occasionally publishes out-of-print defense classics, historical works, and other especially timely or distinguished writing on national security.

NDU Press publications are sold by the U.S. Government Printing Office. For ordering information, call (202) 783-3238 or write to the Superintendent of Documents, U.S. Government Printing Office, Washington, DC 20402.

First Printing, September 1995
Second Printing, April 1997

ISBN 1-57906-025-0

Contents

Part III: Perspectives of Soviet Union Successor States

Part IV: How NATO Must Change

Foreword

NATO Enlargement begins with a review of NATO's origins, development, and expansion experiences. It then examines the usefulness of the Western European Union (WEU) and the Partnership for Peace (PFP) program as paths to NATO membership. It evaluates the efforts of the Visegrad states to achieve membership and presents the perspectives of EU/WEU Associate Partners (Poland, Romania, and Lithuania) in support of NATO enlargement.

The contrary views of successor states of the former Soviet Union (Russia, Ukraine, and Belarus) follow. The Russian government is adamantly opposed to NATO enlargement, arguing that it would be damaging to Russia's economic, political, and military interests, and would isolate Russia. Ukraine supports NATO expansion if it does not exclude or isolate states, or acknowledge any Russian "sphere of influence" over former USSR territory. Belarus argues the need for a European security council that reflects European interests, restricts the sphere of American influence in European affairs, and includes Russia and other former states of the Soviet Union.

Taking up the question of how NATO must change if it is to enlarge, the book considers political, military and defense program requirements. When NATO enlarges, major political changes will become necessary, military command relationships will need to be modified, and defense infrastructure requirements will be enormous. Three conclusions emerge: (1) dramatic progress in the Partnership for Peace program has led to a high degree of self-differentiation among the partner states, and has shifted Central European attitudes toward PFP from one of skepticism to one of enthusiastic support; (2) Expansion would have a very negative impact politically within Russia, damage from which a compensation package will not fully offset; and (3) NATO enlargement will take years to accomplish.

Ervin J. Rokke
Lieutenant General, U.S. Air Force
President, National Defense University

An Overview of *NATO Enlargement*

Jeffrey Simon

Ever since the revolutions of 1989, NATO has been grappling with a Europe in transformation. NATO began its outreach program to the former Warsaw Pact with the July 1990 Declaration. Then, even as the November 1991 Rome NATO Summit adopted a new Strategic Concept to replace its outdated 1967 Flexible Response strategy, NATO was forced to grapple with the task of how to accommodate the East after the collapse of the Warsaw Pact. The Rome Summit also began to face this challenge when it established the North Atlantic Cooperation Council (NACC) to address Europe's eastern security issues.

While the NACC had laudable goals, its limitations immediately became apparent. First, the disintegration of the Soviet Union at the end of 1991 and the decision to include all its successor states as new NACC members meant that rather than the originally conceived five non-Soviet Warsaw Pact members and the USSR, the NACC would include twenty-plus new members. The immense diversity among NACC partners (e.g., between Poland and Uzbekistan) led to demands for differentiation, and increasing demands for Alliance membership by many NACC members. In sum, despite well-intended goals, the cooperation partners' demands on the NACC made it quite apparent how ill-prepared the organization really was. NATO's most recent response came in January 1994 when the North Atlantic Council adopted the Partnership for Peace (PFP) program and the Combined Joint Task Force (CJTF).

NATO's responses to developments in the East—first, to the former Warsaw Pact members and second, to the successor states emerging from the disintegrated Soviet Union, former Yugoslavia, and Czechoslovakia—have been extraordinary in that so many new initiatives have been taken in such a short time. They have been insufficient in that events have moved at such a fast pace that NATO's responses have not kept up with expectations in the region.

NATO Enlargement, which resulted from a conference sponsored by

1

the Institute for National Strategic Studies (INSS), National Defense University, is divided into four parts. **Part I** examines the guidelines and paths of NATO enlargement; how enlargement has occurred historically, how enlargement might occur through the European Union (EU)/Western European Union (WEU) path, and finally through the Partnership for Peace (PFP). **Part II** examines the implications of NATO enlargement from the perspectives of three WEU Associated Partners—Poland, Romania, and Lithuania. **Part III** examines NATO enlargement implications from three successor states of the Former Soviet Union (FSU)—Russia, Ukraine, and Belarus. **Part IV** discusses various aspects of how the Alliance needs to change to accommodate new members; what political adjustments, military command alterations, and military infrastructure changes will be necessary.

Part I
The Paths to NATO Enlargement

Previous NATO enlargements have derived from different circumstances and reasons. Lawrence Kaplan in Chapter 1 notes that after the initial decision in March 1948 to include the United States and Canada with the Western Union "core"—U.K., France, and Benelux—the United States insisted that NATO also include "peripheral" members Norway, Iceland, Portugal, Denmark, and Italy because they shared common values and were needed for geo-strategic reasons. Indeed, Norway and Denmark accepted membership with hesitations, the latter with a "footnote" that neither atomic weapons nor allied military forces would be stationed on their territory.

It was the Korean War that provided the catalyst for the entrance of Greece and Turkey, who had been excluded in 1948. At the September 1950 North Atlantic Council meeting in New York, Greece and Turkey became associate members allowing them to participate in defense planning; they became full members at the Lisbon Conference in 1952.

When the Federal Republic of Germany joined in 1955, NATO was transformed into a military organization and Germany agreed to limits on its force levels and restrictions on the manufacture of weapons of mass destruction. When post-Franco Spain entered the Alliance in 1982 it refused to participate in the integrated military command, but sought membership to strengthen democracy and provide Spain with the opportunity to enter the European Economic Community (now European Union). Finally, in 1990 when the former German Democratic Republic became part of a unified Germany, the four-plus-two agreement restricted NATO military presence and activities in Germany's five eastern laender (states) until the last Russian troops left in the Fall of 1994. In sum, previous NATO enlargements have been driven by common values, geographic and defense requirements, and have included restrictions on new members.

Jean Félix-Paganon argues in Chapter 2 that future NATO enlargement is not likely to occur through the path of the European Union (EU) and its West European Union (WEU); and that memberships in the EU, WEU, and NATO should converge.

Based on the Brussels Treaty of 1948 and modified by the Paris Agreements in 1954, the WEU was reactivated in 1987 with the Platform on European Security Interests; and by participating in the Iran-Iraq War and Gulf War. The December 1991 Maastrict decisions defined the WEU's consultation and operational role. At Maastrict, the WEU also issued a separate declaration to offer full membership or associate status to other EU members and associate membership to other non-EU European-NATO states.

In the June 1992 Petersburg Declaration the WEU's operational role was strengthened. For the WEU, the January 1994 NATO Brussels summit was important politically, in that all allies—including the United States—recognized that a European defense was compatible with NATO; and militarily, in that the Alliance would provide its assets in the form of CJTFs.

The WEU has made further efforts to project stability to Central and Eastern Europe. In 1992 it established a Consultation Forum and in 1994 a status of association was established with nine associate partners; the four Visegrad states, the three Baltic states, Bulgaria and Romania. The prospects for WEU's enlargement are dependent on developments in other organizations: the EU and NATO. The EU has agreed that the next phase of enlargement should begin only after the Intergovernmental Conference (IGC) in 1996 and that since all three organizations (EU, WEU, and NATO) must take into account the different requirements of each organization; that in the long run, the European memberships of the three organizations should converge. In sum, the WEU has already drawn lines in Europe and decided that its enlargement will not precede

NATO's.

As I argue in Chapter 3, future candidates for NATO membership are likely to be drawn from among the 26 states participating in the Partnership for Peace program established in January 1994. While we do not know precisely how the Alliance will enlarge (presently being developed in NATO's draft study directed by the December 1, 1994 NAC) nor what the Alliance will approve as necessary conditions for membership, it is likely that they will include:

- active participation in NACC and the Partnership program
- the successful performance of democratic political institutions
- a free market economy
- respect for human rights.

It is also likely that effective democratic control of the military as well as some minimal degree of military capability and NATO interoperability will be necessary conditions.

NATO's challenge, though, will be how to define and decide what constitutes "effective" democratic control of the military, recognizing that each state has its own history, culture, and unique set of institutions. The current state of civil-military relations among those Central European (Visegrad) states, frequently referred to as the most likely to join NATO first, were examined according to the following four elements.

1) A clear division of authority between the president and government (prime minister and defense minister) in constitutions, amendments, or through public law. The law should clearly establish who commands and controls the military and promotes senior military officers in peacetime, who holds emergency powers in crisis, and who has authority for the transition to war.

2) Parliamentary oversight of the military through control of the defense budget. Parliament's role in deploying armed forces in emergency and war must be clear.

3) Peacetime government control of general staffs and military commanders through civilian defense ministries. Control should include preparation of the defense budget, access to intelligence, involvement

in strategic planning, force structure development, arms acquisitions and deployments, and military promotions.

4) Restoration of military prestige, trustworthiness and accountability for the armed forces to be effective. Having come from the communist period when the military was often used as an instrument of external or internal oppression, society must perceive the military as being under effective government control. Military training levels and equipment must be sufficient to national defense requirements.

If NATO deems these four conditions necessary for effective democratic control of the military, then most of the Visegrad states would *not* yet qualify. Although Central Europe has already made enormous progress in civil-military relations since the 1989 revolutions, it is clear that much work remains to be done and that Partnership for Peace can play an important role in preparing aspiring candidates to membership.

Part II
Perspectives of European Union/
Western European Union Associate Partners

According to Andrzej Karkoszka in Chapter 4, the 1989 revolutions ended the period of Poland's domination, but marked a return to the period before 1939. **Poland** wants full membership in NATO, not just for the military factor, but because it seeks internal transformation and engagement with all other Western institutions. On the one hand, Poland feels no immediate threats; it has successfully developed good relations with its seven neighbors. On the other hand, Poland has some long-term external security concerns to the East; particularly with Russia, which has been sliding back to its classic security doctrine since the Fall of 1993. Therefore, Central Europe's (and Poland's) integration in NATO provides a hedge against future pressures from Russia.

Karkoszka outlines four alternative security options for Poland. Either Poland can rebuild links with Russia to restore her security guarantee; pursue neutrality and self-defense; build a regional security system with small- and medium-sized neighboring states; or pursue integration into the Euro-Atlantic security system. Within the fourth, and most favored option, exist several parallel paths of action to include engaging the EU, WEU, and NATO and pursuing bilateral and trilateral forms of cooperation.

Initially, Poland viewed PFP with apprehension, but now views it with enthusiasm for its integrating and interoperability aspects. PFP's one weakness, though, is that it prolongs the process and contributes to Poland's impatience because of the urgent need to modernize its forces. On the positive side, Poland sees PFP participation as: the *only* means to NATO membership, an efficient means to promote regional stability, and permitting self-differentiation, which has gone much further than originally planned. Poland's problems with democratic control of its armed forces result from growing pains. Karkoszka argues that even if Poland is excluded from among NATO's first PFP entrants, it will continue to pursue active participation.

Romania, according to Ioan Mircea Pascu in Chapter 5, entered the post-Cold War era with false expectations. Originally, Romania believed that the CSCE process could replace the loss of the Warsaw Pact. Romania has changed its attitude and seeks inclusion in enlarged Western institutions—the EU/WEU and NATO. Romania is a WEU Associate Partner, but sees the U.S. presence in Europe and NATO as indispensable for security. Pascu argues that NATO is simultaneously performing two functions: it remains a military alliance for its 16 members, *and* it acts as an embryo security organization to deal with a wide variety of security risks for partners.

Romania wants NATO to clarify the PFP process and define its relationship to enlargement; the "how" and "who" questions. Will admission be by individual or group? What criteria will be applied? After describing the advantages and disadvantages of NATO's enlargement options—moving either east or southeast, Pascu then explains the benefits of what he calls a "checkers approach" enlargement option. If Romania and Poland (the "checkers")—the two most important states by population, armed forces, and geo-strategic location—became de jure members of NATO, Ukraine and other Central European states would automatically become de facto members.

Pascu then explained that Romania's willingness to sign PFP represented an effort to overcome the Nicolae Ceausescu legacy that has handicapped Romania in its efforts to integrate into Euro-Atlantic structures. He argues that if Romania were excluded from the initial wave of NATO enlargement that it could have consequences on Romania's internal politics; that it would become very difficult to motivate the Romanian public and electorate that Euro-Atlantic integration is the right policy for Romania.

Eitvydas Bajarunas in Chapter 6 argues that **Lithuania** feels that history has demonstrated that the Baltic states lack the essentials to independently safeguard their national security and sovereignty. That is why Lithuania has made a clear choice to develop good-neighbor relations (e.g., Baltic Council and Baltic Battalion, and close relations with Nordic states) and to join NATO and the EU/WEU.

Bajarunas defines the Baltic states as Central European, but with large Russian minorities and heavy economic dependence on Russia. It has been their fate to lie between Germany and Russia. The main external threats to Lithuania derive from instability in Russia (and in Kaliningrad) and in the Commonwealth of Independent States (CIS). For these reasons, management of relations with Russia is the most serious security challenge facing the Baltic states.

The present Baltic role is to act as a "bridge" between Russia and the West; to prevent Russia's isolation from the West. This requires that NATO develop a *real* strategic partnership with Russia to integrate Russia into the West, but not to overshadow NATO's relations with other partners. This must be complemented with an EU-Russian economic partnership and a strengthened Organization for Security and Cooperation in Europe (OSCE).

For the Baltic states, the NACC and PFP are particularly important in that they provide NATO assistance in forming Baltic military structures that must be built from scratch. At the same time, Bajarunas argues that the NACC is limited and needs to more fully take into account the diversity of partners' needs; and PFP should establish a fund if it is to have active partners who can take advantage of the program.

Lithuania sees PFP as an interim step toward full membership. NATO is seen as a crucial safeguard against the unknown. Russia should have no veto on NATO enlargement. If Lithuania is excluded from the first NATO enlargement, it would need political and psychological reassurance, perhaps in the form of a different future membership commitment such as an associate membership status (with timetable and procedures). Bajarunas argues that if such an arrangement is not found, then enlargement will *reduce* rather than improve European security. In this regard, Lithuania welcomed the 1993 Copenhagen Summit of the EU

Council that recognized that the EU membership of associated states was an objective and the December 1994 Essen Summit that adopted a pre-accession strategy. Lithuania wants and expects NATO to make a similar decision.

Part III
Perspectives of Soviet Union Successor States

Alexei Pushkov argues in Chapter 7 that **Russia** opposes NATO enlargement. He portrays NATO enlargement to include Central and Eastern Europe as the most important and potentially most explosive issue for Russia's foreign policy and to Russian society. It should also be regarded as the ultimate test of Russia's relationship with the West. No other issue—not even disagreements between Moscow and Washington over the sales of a nuclear reactor or conventional armaments to Iran, the lifting of UN sanctions against Iraq, differences over the crisis in Bosnia, nor Russia's military actions in Chenchnya—might harm this relationship so much, should it be accompanied without regard for Russia's deepest worries and frustrations. Seen from Moscow, the outcome of NATO's eastward enlargement will shape the future relationship between Russia and the West.

Russia's nervous reaction is linked to Russia's Cold War image of NATO as a militarist organization. This view prevailed when Hungarian reformers in 1956 and Czechoslovak reformers in 1968 wanted to leave the Warsaw Pact and join NATO. Even when Soviet leaders courted Western leaders during the 1970s and 1980s detente period, NATO was viewed as a militarist, aggressive camp.

During 1991-1993 a romantic period prevailed. Russia largely thought that NATO would change by itself and become involved in disarmament and threats outside Europe. Russia joined NACC and began to establish ties with NATO. By the end of 1992 this changed when it became apparent that the West would not allow Russia a place in their own arms market. During 1993 the issue of NATO enlargement to include the Visegrad states arose; some discussion even included Ukraine and the Baltic states, but all discussion excluded Russia. When Boris Yeltsin strongly opposed NATO enlargement in the Fall of 1993, he reflected the consensus of the entire spectrum of Russian opinion on the question.

With NATO's announcement of Partnership for Peace , four schools of thought developed. One represented by Foreign Minister Kozyrev argued that PFP was a Russian foreign policy achievement and that Russia should join PFP to influence its course of development and prevent Russia's isolation. The second school considered PFP as a NATO dictation toward Russia of a policy that would marginalize Russia and take over its sphere of influence in Europe. This school believes Russia should maintain good relations with China and stay outside the PFP. The third school was concerned that Russia would become one of many partners; hence, this school preferred to stress the need for "equal partnership" with NATO. The fourth school saw PFP as a temporary compromise and saw participation as the first step to deeper interaction with the Alliance. This school called for special status and to conclude a strategic agreement which would guarantee Russian participation without becoming a member of the Alliance. In the end, the foreign ministry compromise was to couple its signature to PFP to a "special status" for Russia. But differences over Bosnian policy began to shake Moscow's hope for a strategic partnership with the Alliance. By December 1994, Kozyrev refused to sign PFP in Brussels and Yeltsin had threatened "Cold Peace" at the OSCE Budapest Summit if NATO enlarged. This marked a new stage in Russia's relations with NATO and coincided with the war in Chenchnya. When NATO began to discuss enlargement in February 1995, the political landscape in Russia had greatly shifted.

Pushkov argues that NATO enlargement will *not* generate a new Cold War because Russia is not in a position to engage in another confrontation. Nevertheless, the consequences would be significant. NATO enlargement would deepen the gap between Russian civilization and the West, result in Russia's inward reorientation, create a rebirth of the Russian sphere of influence among the former states of the Soviet Union, create additional strains between Moscow and Kiev and the Baltic states, destroy START II and CFE, influence domestic politics in favor of anti-Western forces, and encourage a new militarism in Russia.

Pushkov argues that Russia does not need tokenism, but does need the following *real* guarantees from NATO:

1) time guarantees (e.g., no new members before the year 2000)

2) enlargement should not border Russia

3) no deployment of nuclear weapons in Central Europe

4) no forward deployments of military forces

5) NATO should provide Russia with a strategic treaty.

If NATO does provide these five guarantees, it could keep Russia from moving away from the West and achieve gains that would be much greater than any that can be achieved by enlarging NATO eastward.

In Chapter 8, Ihor Kharchenko claims that when **Ukraine** was under the USSR, its July 1990 Declaration on State Sovereignty called for sovereignty, neutrality, and non-nuclear status. After the USSR disintegrated, Ukraine did *not* join the CIS (May 1992), but it did join NATO's NACC. During 1992-1993 Ukraine's ultimate goal was to escape its security vacuum and join European structures.

The legal and political framework for Ukraine's new international security policy was formalized when the Parliament adopted a Foreign Policy Concept in July 1993 that supported Ukraine's participation in existing institutions (OSCE, NACC, NATO, and the WEU) with the goal of creating all-European security structures. Also Ukraine's October 1993 Military Doctrine modified Ukraine's former neutrality to the new conditions and declared Ukraine's intention to join Western institutions.

Ukraine's goal is to build a new united Europe on the principle of "indivisibility of security." In the NACC Ukraine argued for nuclear power security guarantees in return for eliminating nuclear weapons on its soil and acceding to NPT. Differences between Ukraine and the Central and East European applicants for NATO membership exist not in political philosophy, but rather in practicalities, formalities, and geographic realities. Hence, Ukraine criticizes the WEU's (6+3) associate partner program as too "exclusive" and applauds PFP as inclusive (Ukraine was one of the program's first signatories and remains an active participant in its programs). As a result, Ukraine's participation in NACC and PFP did not cause the strong political debate in Ukrainian society that it did in Russia.

Ukraine's position on NATO enlargement includes the fact that it has never renounced the idea of joining NATO, that "no veto" should be exercised by any state, and that European security is mainly characterized by the parallel existence of NATO and the CIS. Ukraine's main concern is that it might become a "buffer state" between an unstable CIS and an enlarged NATO. Since Central and Eastern Europe (to which Ukraine belongs) want to join NATO, Ukraine would like NATO to broaden from a classic-type collective defense system to a collective security organization that is the nucleus of a future all-European security system.

Hence, Ukraine (in marked contrast to Russia) accepted NATO enlargement and sees this as neither a speedy, nor momentous process. Time is needed to prevent overburdening the unstable political situation in the Newly Independent States (NIS) and to allow NATO to evolve its new role in an all-European security system. For this reason, Ukraine wants NATO's relations with Russia to remain cordial so that Russia is not isolated. Ukraine, though, sees Russia's demands forbidding NATO enlargement to Ukraine and the Baltic states as a negative process.

While Ukraine has not yet applied for NATO membership, it wants to work out the modalities of a "special relationship" with the Alliance beyond the framework of NACC and PFP. Ukraine seeks closer and mutually beneficial ties with Russia and her immediate neighbors to the west (i.e., Hungary, Moldova, Poland, Romania, and Slovakia) as well as to expand relations with the West. But, Ukraine's main ties with the West are bilateral and its only multilateral security tie is NACC.

In the end, NATO's relationship to Ukraine and Russia will be different. Russia is part of the CIS and Ukraine is not. Russia is a nuclear power and Ukraine is implementing START I and approaching *de facto* non-nuclear status. Ukraine's security concept is based on the principles of "indivisibility of security:" inclusiveness, openness, and transparency. Kharchenko argues that in the long-term, deliberations on NATO enlargement, together with OSCE discussions on a security model should lead to a more comprehensive future European security architecture.

Belarus, according to Anatol Maisenia in Chapter 9, was neutral in 1993, but now is solidly under Russia's influence and closely follows the CIS. This change, though, is *not* due to NATO enlargement, but to the fact that Russia is in the process of revival and Belarus naturally falls within Russia's sphere of influence. Belarus renegotiated its May 1993 treaty with Russia and provides the litmus test of Russia's policies in the Near Abroad.

Instead of the stability and predictability of the former communist era, the threats to security are instability and unpredictability which results from the break-up of the former USSR, division of military equipment based on the territorial principle, and degeneration of national liberation and democratic movements into extreme nationalism in regions where anti-Russian attitudes prevail.

In this environment, it is necessary to construct a new European security system. The shortest route to this end is to open a European perspective for the NIS and include them in the common European economic space. The aim is to create a multiple-level system of collective security with the NACC and OSCE. Under OSCE, Maisenia suggests creating a European Security Council with a military-political organization to carry out its resolutions. With NATO's effort to revalidate its new role, NATO must be widened to bring Russia and other NIS into its structure. Since the new European architecture will need to comprise "vertical" and "horizontal" dimensions (in contrast to the Cold War "vertical" poles), Belarus' neutrality makes no sense, resulting in only self-isolation. Belarus must participate in regional organizations such as the Baltic Council, the Black Sea Union, and NATO-bis.

Partnership for Peace was a good policy because it represented NATO's recognition that enlargement would not promote European stability, but undermine it. It reinforced European integration, prevented creating a "*cordon sanitaire*," and recognized the impact of enlargement on Russia's political scene. In sum, the West recognized that it was more important to preserve Russia's readiness to cooperate and move toward reform than give instant security guarantees to Central and East European states.

PFP is a multi-speed arrangement; for Central and Eastern Europe, PFP is a route to membership and can provide an open door to Russia and Belarus. If Central Europe had been admitted into NATO too early, it would have driven Belarus to Russia in common opposition to the West. PFP has provided Belarus the opportunity to cooperate with *both* West and East. Nevertheless, democratic values should remain the basic criteria for PFP; hence, PFP should *not* be blind to violations in Russia and Belarus if they occur.

Part IV
How NATO Must Change

Hans Jochen Peters argues in Chapter 10 that the enlargement of

NATO is the most significant **political decision** that the Alliance has had to face since the Dual Track decision of 1979 and will involve consequences that are as yet unforeseeable. This is the reason why NATO in December 1994 engaged in its study on "how" enlargement is to proceed; to build a consensus among the 16 member-states and develop a common set of arguments in the forthcoming ratification debate.

NATO's political transformation began with the Rome Summit in November 1991 and the creation of the NACC. This was followed by the January 1994 Brussels Summit that launched Partnership for Peace. These decisions began the process of NATO's political transformation to the new international environment. All of this must be achieved without compromising or diluting NATO's existing capacity.

Though political motivations were present in previous NATO enlargements in 1952, 1955, and 1982, security-related interests were predominant. Contemporary NATO enlargement involves a larger number of states (roughly ten) who seek not just protection, but who stress more the sharing of common values and the political motivation to belong to the West. Citing Richard Holbrooke, Peters argues the forthcoming enlargement constitutes Europe's "fourth architectural moment" (following 1815, 1919, and the late 1940s).

Though NATO's export of stability by enlargement will unavoidably mean a certain degree of instability, new members cannot blackball others seeking membership; they must transcend the unresolved ethnic and border problems resulting from the post-World War I Versailles, Trianon, and Saint Germain treaties. New members must also be prepared to support NATO's policies including aiding those remaining outside the Alliance, cooperating with Russia, and contributing to OSCE and UN peacekeeping missions. Since further enlargement will be part of building a new security structure, it must *not* lead to NATO's dilution as a "hard" security agency to a "weak" collective security institution.

After enlargement, NATO faces a number of political tasks that include the need to:

1) forge a new trans-Atlantic bargain (e.g., CJTF)

2) focus on NATO's five southern members (e.g., Mediterranean initiative)

3) organize relations with those partners excluded from the first wave of

enlargement (e.g., NACC allows political cooperation and PFP military cooperation under Article 4)

4) deal with the likely new problems created by enlargement (e.g., specifically how to find the means to establish relations with Russia).

Despite the many political and internal problems resulting from enlargement, Peters concludes that NATO's decision will prove to be historically correct.

In Chapter 11 Catherine Kelleher argues that the **military dimensions** of NATO enlargement require that any new member should have full rights and obligations of an Alliance member. In other words, Articles 4 and 5 will apply for new members. There will be no second class members of the Alliance.

NATO's November 1991 Strategic Concept provides overall guidance for NATO's military structures that will arise out of enlargement. First, it says that we will face new risks in quantity and quality. We must expect minor military contingencies or ethnic problems that will require conventional military forces, and can assume long warning times and pre-conflict stages to allow for political negotiation. Another assumption is that NATO defines itself as having no adversary.

These changed assumptions require NATO's military transformation in the areas of force dispersion, differentiation, and coordination. With NATO's enlargement, peacetime deployment and stationing will have to be determined by the new member and the Alliance. However, certainly during times of crisis or war, the Alliance must retain the right of transit and stationing on the territory of any new member.

Because NATO has smaller active duty rapid reaction forces, this creates different military requirements for mobilization of reserves and dispersion of military forces. These same requirements will fall on new NATO members as well. Finally, coordinating forces by the integrated military structure, the *sine qua non* for military effectiveness, will be challenged. NATO must look at new adaptations for headquarters, simplify command structures (perhaps along the lines of CJTF), and re-examine theater air defenses and ballistic missile defenses.

Independent of the precise new members and their particular military needs, Kelleher argues that NATO has a number of instruments to guide NATO's military transformation. These include the CJTF concept, which provides flexibility and effectiveness against an uncertain threat; the Planning and Review Process (PARP), a modified version of the Defense Planning Questionnaires (DPQ) for humanitarian assistance, search and rescue, and peacekeeping operations. In addition, in bilateral channels the United States has linked national guard and reserve units on a state-by-state basis with partners, and a Joint Air Traffic Control Management System that has been expanded to most of Central and Eastern Europe.

Richard Kugler notes in Chapter 12 that the **defense program requirements** of NATO enlargement are significant because they are much larger than just military infrastructure. The defense program will need to create a new command structure, upgrade forces of new members to be compatible with NATO forces, and improve the capacity of NATO forces to work with those of new members.

The act of enlarging NATO will create two-way commitments that go far beyond present NACC and PFP activities. Enlargement is more than just a political act; it is also a security and military step. Article 5 commitments require corresponding partner commitments and NATO must avoid hollow political commitments. If NATO enlarges to include the four Visegrad states, it will take about twenty years in steady step-by-step efforts to upgrade new member forces and NATO's forces to work with them. Kugler notes that it took between 1975-1995 to achieve Rationalization, Standardization, and Interoperability (RSI) for NATO forces.

The costs will vary with the force goals and military horizons that NATO sets for itself. If NATO decides to merely configure new members' forces to defend themselves with NATO help only in C^3I and logistics support, the cost will be relatively low. If NATO decides to supplement this commitment with sizable combat forces from Western Europe, then the cost will rise, particularly if military infrastructure is developed in the East. Depending on the choice, the ten-year out-of-pocket expenses could vary between $10-50 billion, with $35 billion as a mid-range estimate.

In all likelihood NATO will not be able to afford, much less need, the permanent stationing of large combat forces in Central and Eastern Europe in peacetime. Because new member forces were in the Warsaw Pact, which stressed offensive large highly-regimented ground operations, they will be difficult to harmonize with NATO operations, which emphasizes defensive joint air-ground, maneuver, high tech, and individual initiative. Not only will the tasks facing new NATO members be great, they will be required to carry their fair share of the burden. In addition, new members will lack the resources to upgrade their postures and infrastructure to meet NATO standards. Not only will this take money, it will take time and it will limit how new members operate with NATO forces. A variety of models for integrating new member forces with NATO exists; these range from deep integration (e.g., AFCENT during the Cold War) to a relatively mild integration (e.g., CJTFs for single operations).

NATO, which has been designed to defend Alliance borders, must become skilled at a projection strategy and developing forces that possess deployment, mobile logistics, transportation, and service support assets to carry out the mission. Not only do NATO forces need to be restructured for out-of-area projection, but if NATO decides that we need to deploy POMCUS sets, air bases, ground reception facilities, training sites, and base small combat forces on the territory of new members, costs could escalate. Hence, NATO's ultimate aim must be to operate its forces side-by-side with partners, rather than intermeshing with them.

Kugler argues that for the four Visegrad states a ten-year investment strategy of roughly $35 billion is necessary in order to prevent a hollow NATO enlargement that leaves everybody no better off than before, and possibly far worse for the wear.

Conclusions

1) Previous NATO enlargements have not only been driven by common values, geography, and defense requirements, they have also included restrictions on new members. Hence, future enlargements could establish necessary conditions such as democratic control of the military and restrictions prohibiting new members from blackballing others seeking membership.

2) Projected time-lines for NATO enlargement are not likely to occur before the year 2000 for the Visegrad states. Accelerated enlargement can have negative consequences on European stability and security. It is necessary for the EU/WEU Associated Partners program and NATO's Partnership for Peace to take hold to stabilize the situation

for those states initially excluded.

3) When NATO expands, the EU/WEU will provide some stability and security to those associated partners *not* included in the first group to join NATO. Nevertheless, compensation through deepening PFP and enriching NACC or developing more clearly defined paths (e.g., associate membership?) will likely be necessary.

4) Compensating former Soviet Union states not in the EU/WEU associate partners program will likely be more difficult. When NATO enlarges, these states will experience enormous insecurity and instability. Hence, NATO must compensate for this by enriched PFP programs, NACC enhancements, or other (treaty?) arrangements.

5) It is clear that when NATO enlarges, the Alliance will have to change. The political dimensions of enlargement will be challenging, the military dimensions will be complex, and the defense program requirements costly.

Part I

The Path to NATO Enlargement

---

1 Historical Aspects
Lawrence S. Kaplan

2 The Western European Union Path
Jean Félix-Paganon

3 The Partnership For Peace Path and Civil-Military Relations
Jeffrey Simon

DR. LAWRENCE S. KAPLAN

Dr. Kaplan is University Professor Emeritus of History and Director Emeritus of the Lyman L. Lemnitzer Center for NATO and European Community Studies at Kent State University. He is currently Adjunct Professor of History at Georgetown University. Prior to his position at Kent State, he was with the Historical Office, Office of the Secretary of Defense. He has written numerous articles, monographs, and books on U.S. diplomatic history and NATO affairs, including A Community of Interests: NATO and the Military Assistance Program, 1948-1951 (1980), The United States and NATO: The Formative Years (1984), (ed.) American Historians and the Atlantic Alliance (1991), and NATO and the United States: The Enduring Alliance (1988; updated edition, 1994).

Historical Aspects
1

Lawrence S. Kaplan

Since NATO's Brussels summit adopted Partnership for Peace (PFP) in January 1994, the prospect of enlarging the alliance by admitting new members, particularly Poland, the Czech Republic, and Hungary, has been a major concern of the Atlantic allies. NATO pressed by the United States has been preoccupied with the consequences of new relationships, whether as "partners" or full members.[1]

Such questions as the scope of enlargement, the impact on Russia, and the terms of admission are not yet resolved. Nor has the larger question of the meaning of NATO in light of projected enlargement been settled. What can be answered in this period of gestation is what happened during NATO's first two generations as a result of enlargement in 1949 when the "stepping stone" nations were accepted; in 1952 when Greece and Turkey joined the alliance; in 1955 when the Federal Republic of Germany entered NATO; and in 1982 when Spain became the sixteenth member.

Since its conception in 1948, the composition of its membership has been a problem for the Atlantic alliance. If NATO was an instrument of American imperial power, as political scientist David Calleo proclaimed a generation ago, it was also an "empire by invitation," as Norwegian historian Geir Lundestad suggests.[2] The inspiration for the alliance was European not American. Worried about the rising tide of Soviet-led communism, anxious Western Europeans insisted upon an American guarantee of their security, threatened as it appeared to be by internal Communist subversion and by external Soviet intimidation. While the United States had recognized the fragility of European economies through the Marshall Plan of 1947, economic aid was not sufficient of itself. Economic recovery would be unlikely if it were not accompanied by a sense of security which only an entangling tie with the United States would confer.

The Western Union "core". America's response initially was hesitant, despite bipartisan concern for the containment of Communism and the revival of Europe. An entangling alliance would repudiate a tradition of non-entanglement beginning with the termination of the Franco-American alliance in the eighteenth century. It might also give Europe a license to raid the American treasury by turning over its defense preparations to the United States. To obviate this criticism Britain's Foreign Minister Ernest Bevin, in association with France's Foreign Minister Georges Bidault, and colleagues in the Benelux countries, signed the Brussels Pact in March 1948, establishing the Western Union to meet American demands of self-help and mutual cooperation.

Ideally, the Western Union countries would have preferred the United States to join their association. But recognizing the continuing pull of American isolationism, they were able, with the help of American supporters in the Congress and administration, to remove the stigma of entanglement by the semantic device of an "Atlantic label" and by bringing Canada into the alliance. In the lengthy negotiations in Washington in the summer of 1948 the European allies were required to make concessions to win the American "pledge" under Article 5 of the North Atlantic Treaty, wherein "An armed attack against one or more of them in Europe or North America shall be considered an attack against them all."

To achieve this objective the European partners in the Western Union had to agree to expand the alliance in accordance with American concerns, something not in the plans of the Brussels Pact nations that had negotiated the terms of the Treaty of Washington. They wished instead to confine European membership to their own ranks.

"Peripheral" members. American demands to include Norway, Iceland, and Portugal were initially resisted on the grounds that Norway's interests differed from Belgium's or Holland's, while Iceland and Portugal were hardly part of Europe at all, even though they fit into an Atlantic context. And Italy and Denmark were objectionable, if only because of their distance from the Atlantic. What the Europeans did not admit directly was their unwillingness to share American military and economic support, which would be by-products of political commitment, with outlying nations. Eelco van Kleffens of the Netherlands offered a solution—second-class membership to non-Western Union allies. The alliance he recommended would resemble "a peach, the Brussels Pact would be the hard kernel in the center and a North Atlantic Pact the somewhat less hard mass around it."[3]

The core members only grudgingly accepted what they called "peripheral" members to perform specific tasks but not to share decision-making authority. None of these reservations was acceptable to the senior partner, although in practice some of the peripheral members in fact limited their own contributions to the alliance for their own reasons. Iceland had no standing army, nor any intentions of creating one. Portugal was wary of any European integration that would complicate its relations with Spain.

Norway and Denmark accepted membership with some hesitations—Denmark more than Norway, but also with the understanding that a "footnote," as it came to be identified, assured that neither atomic weapons nor allied military forces would be stationed on their territory. Fear of repercussions from the Soviet Union not doubts about American pledges accounted for this footnote. But neither doubts on the part of the peripheral members nor antagonism on the part of the Brussels partners deterred the United States from pressing its case for bringing Norway, Denmark and Portugal into the alliance. The explanation lay in Norway's Spitzbergen, Denmark's Greenland and Portugal's Azores as vital strategic locations for American participation in the defense of Europe. The islands guarded Atlantic sea lanes and would serve along with Iceland as bases for American aircraft enroute to Europe.

Italy, however, was another matter. Initially, the Western Union powers had no more interest in bringing Italy into NATO than they had the Scandinavian countries. Moreover, Italy suffered more disabilities as a potential member than the Nordic nations. Its geographic location was far from the Atlantic, and the terms of the 1947 peace treaty with Italy would restrict its military development. A strong Communist presence was another obstacle in the way of membership. If Italy was able to surmount these disabilities, it was in part through the role of John Hickerson, director of the State Department's Office of European Affairs.

From the beginnings of negotiation Hickerson served as a "grey eminence" quietly impressing diplomats with the importance of preventing Italy from loss to future Communist control. He first overcame objections from the Joint Chiefs of Staff to overextending commitments in the Mediterranean, and then from senior American diplomats. As for the Europeans, France's early hesitations evaporated as it insisted on Italy in the alliance as a balance to Norway. The French ambassador in London informed Ernest Bevin it was unlikely that France would ratify the treaty "if Norway was a member of it and Italy not."[4] France was determined to ensure that the northern Europeans would not dominate the European side of the Atlantic. Such were the complicated nine-month negotiations over the North Atlantic Treaty.

Greece and Turkey Excluded. Italy's accession to NATO inevitably raised Greek and Turkish hopes of joining the alliance. If Italy, a former Axis partner geographically removed from the Atlantic, could become a member of NATO, why should other anti-Communist nations bordering the Mediterranean be excluded? Greece and Turkey had other claims as well. They had been the initial potential victims of Soviet enlargementism, from their own perspective, and initial beneficiaries of the Truman Doctrine in 1947. It made sense that membership in the Western alliance would anchor the security which both nations were seeking in 1949. If Italy was acceptable to the allies, then the important strategic position of Turkey along with its considerable military potential should have been welcomed by the NATO partners.

While Greece lacked the military potential to assist the alliance, it held a special place in American foreign policy because the Greek civil war had become a symbol in the United States of resistance to Communism. The United States had extended the initial Greek-Turkish aid program of 1947 by an appropriation of $25 million for fiscal year 1949. The American investment psychologically and economically was heavy, as the American mission in Athens under General James Van Fleet was the effective bulwark against the Communist opponents. In the American mind Greece and Turkey stood in the way of Soviet enlargement in southeastern Europe. For the Joint Chiefs of Staff, Turkey in particular, could be a valued ally, with its strong national spirit and geographic situation. At Pentagon conversations in March 1948, the United States and Great Britain did not include either country in a projected Atlantic security arrangement but planned to issue a joint declaration pledging to uphold the independence and territorial integrity of Greece, Turkey, and Iran. Given the efforts of Greek-Americans and the special visibility of Greece's plight, Greece if not Turkey should have been as reasonable a candidate for membership as Italy. No invitation, however, was forthcoming. Inevitably, there was opposition on the part of all the European allies to extending the scope of the alliance, even as they recognized that both Greece and Turkey would share such military aid as the United States would grant in the future. Eventually, even empathetic Americans recognized the problem of overextension of commitment and the importance of concentrating on Western Europe. So, Greece and

Turkey were rebuffed in 1949.

Greece and Turkey (1952). The Korean conflict changed American, if not European, perceptions of a potential role of Greece and Turkey in NATO. The unusual comity between the two usually hostile nations was a factor in making them more attractive partners; the June 1948 defection of Yugoslavia from the Soviet bloc produced a Balkan Pact among the three neighbors which lasted throughout the Korean war. But the major attraction was a consequence of the reorganization of NATO. The invasion of South Korea was a reminder to the United States and its allies that the pledge of military assistance—particularly at the modest levels of 1949 and 1950—was insufficient to deter Communist-inspired aggression. NATO required a military presence on the ground to inhibit the Soviets from testing Allied resolve in a divided Germany as they presumably were doing in divided Korea. The result was to transform the treaty into a military organization which would be capable of defending Europe against attack from the east. If the Russians could act through North Koreans or Communist Chinese, they could also employ East Germans as their surrogates. To prevent such an outcome in the fall of 1950, NATO, under the leadership of General Eisenhower as Supreme Allied Commander, Europe, planned to organize Europe into defensible regions. In this context Greece and Turkey on the southeastern flank of NATO became strategic assets rather than embarrassing applicants for membership.

When Greece and Turkey made their first formal applications for membership, they received only the firm support of Italy. The northern members were concerned about assuming responsibility for defending a region distant geographically and culturally from the West. Britain preferred the establishment of a separate Middle East command in which a British commander would group the Balkans with friendly Arab states.

These considerations dissolved in the summer of 1950 under the heat of the Korean conflict and the fears it inspired among Western Europeans. At the September 1950 meeting of the North Atlantic Council (NAC) in New York, the members decided to accord Greece and Turkey associate membership, allowing them to participate in defense planning relating to the Mediterranean. When the Supreme Headquarters, Allied Powers Europe (SHAPE) command was established in December the United States cast its influential vote behind the joint entry of Greece and Turkey in order to secure the southern flank of the SHAPE Command and to establish American air bases in Turkey. In May 1951 the United States proposed full membership, and, as the Iranian crisis mounted that summer the British agreed. Although the Scandinavian allies' approval was reluctant, the North Atlantic Council unanimously recommended the accession of Greece and Turkey at its September 1951 meeting in Ottawa, and formal entry at the Lisbon meeting in February 1952.

For the moment, the deep divisions between Greece and Turkey were subsumed under fear of a common enemy. Whatever doubts the other allies had about the new members' stability were swept away by the consideration of the 25 divisions which Turkey would be able to supply to NATO's southern flank. Visions of the Soviet Union pressing the Turks in eastern Turkey or reigniting the Greek Civil War preparatory to moving against the Dardanelles thrust aside doubts about admitting two nations with a history of hostility to each other and with concerns over the unresolved differences over Cyprus. The Korean war remained the probable opening gambit in the Soviet Union's long-term plans for Europe. NATO's evolution once again was shaped by the perceived defense needs of the alliance.

Federal Republic of Germany (1955). If controversy attended the entry of the 13th and 14th members of NATO, the accession of the 15th, the Federal Republic of Germany, was by far the most difficult as well as the most necessary in the view of the senior partner. The contest between the United States and the Soviet Union over Germany had been central to the Cold War from its inception. It was no coincidence that the Federal Republic grew out of Bizonia and Trizonia, the monetarized Anglo-American-French zones of occupied Germany. Nor is it a coincidence that the Federal Republic itself came into being a month after the North Atlantic Treaty was signed. While it may be an exaggeration to assert that American postwar policy centered on the reconstruction of Germany, it was obvious that the reconstruction of Europe itself, economically as well as militarily, required the incorporation of German resources. Germany was the unstated major issue in every meeting of the allies and in most planning sessions within the United States, even as it was excluded from membership in the alliance.

The linkage of Germany and NATO was made clear in Dean Acheson's conviction as early as April 1949 that the success of negotiations for a German state had been facilitated by the conclusion of the North Atlantic Treaty.[5] The attraction of German membership was self-evident, both in terms of the resources Germans could bring to the alliance and the restraints an Atlantic community might impose on a rehabilitated Germany.

Congress was willing. On the crassest level, Senator Arthur Watkins noted at the treaty ratification hearings that German membership would force Germans to contribute their fair share of the cost to the common effort. After all, Germans would be the beneficiary of Western defense under any circumstance. As the senator put it: "We certainly are not going to fight all their battles for them."[6] In the course of these hearings, John Foster Dulles, the leading Republican foreign policy spokesman, offered another reason for considering German membership: namely, that it would inhibit German temptation to use its geographic position as a bargaining chip between East and West, thus inhibiting a Rapallo-like rapprochement with the Soviet Union in the manner of the Weimar Republic.[7] In executive session, Senator Arthur Vandenberg suggested to fellow senators that German membership would dissolve French fears of Germany.[8]

There were limits to how far public discourse could extend when the issue of German membership arose. The memories of Nazi bestiality were too recent and too strong to expect that the European partners would accept a German national presence in their midst, no matter how rational the arguments might be. This barrier was well understood by the Truman administration and by the Senate as well. Despite a recognition of the advantages inclusion of Germany into NATO might afford, there was no call to action by the Senate Foreign Relations Committee. The language on the German issue had been carefully modulated at the Senate hearings on the Atlantic alliance. Its spokesmen were cautious. Former Under Secretary of State Robert Lovett noted that while Germany was discussed in the treaty negotiations, "We found that its circumstances at the present time make it impossible to be considered as a participant."[9] As the most influential administration spokesman testifying, Secretary of State Acheson begged the question. When asked if the inclusion of western Germany would improve the strategic position of the Atlantic powers, he claimed that he was no military expert but, "Quite clearly at the present time a discussion of including western Germany in the pact is not possible."[10]

The most that the administration could say in public was that Germany's relations with NATO could be reevaluated after the dismantling of German industry had been completed and the elimination of vestiges of Nazism eradicated. Even as the Allies recognized the importance of German manpower in coping with superior Soviet ground forces, the language of denial remained in place. As the House Foreign Affairs Committee deliberated on extending military aid to Europe more than a year after the signing of the pact, Secretary Acheson claimed (in June 1950) that demilitarization of West Germany remained a keystone of American policy: "There is no discussion of anything else . . . That is our policy and we have not raised or revalued it."[11]

While Acheson was technically accurate in his statement of policy, there was full recognition among the allies that the 12 divisions at NATO's disposal in Europe required a German contribution to make a credible defense posture. Position papers in the State Department reflected this concern. As early as November 1949, one paper observed,: "The German problem must be viewed and dealt with in the total context of general developments. It cannot be isolated. What we do in Germany must not be dictated by considerations of what the Germans demand, or even of our respective national interests, but by a fair appraisal of the indispensable requirements of the Western community of free peoples."[12]

The outbreak of the Korean War permitted these confidential communications to be made public, and to generate pressures to counteract the general allied revulsion against the remilitarization of Germany. The leitmotifs of de-Nazification, democratization, and demilitarization were subsumed in the summer of 1950 under a generalized fear that Stalin was planning a similar action in a divided Germany as that in a divided Korea. The specter of 60,000 East German paramilitary troops, backed by 27 Soviet divisions in the eastern zone, galvanized American planners. Instead of a progressive build-up of Western forces, as projected in the May 1950 meeting of the North Atlantic Council, the United States prepared for a massive armament throughout the alliance. Military aid would be increased four-fold, and U.S. forces in Europe would be reinforced. The United States intended to keep its pledge to Europeans.

But such satisfaction as Europeans felt over American activity had to be weighed against the price they would have to pay for America's help. It would be high, particularly if in reciprocation, the European partners would have to concur in the rearmament of Germany. It seemed illogical to congressmen to exclude German resources from the common defense. Germany after all would be protected with Allied manpower and equipment, and so Germans should share the burdens. This line of reasoning was so obvious to Americans that Secretary Acheson had difficulty defending allied defense plans that did not include a German component. But once the immediate threat of a Soviet attack in Germany receded,

Europeans, particularly the French, made clear their reluctance to countenance a revival of their neighbor. The psychic cost of a German army in being only five years after the end of World War II inspired massive French resistance. Yet Europeans had no choice. American pressure was ultimately irresistible, particularly in light of the manifest inability of the West to mount a credible defense without German assistance.

The immediate solution in the difficult fall of 1950 was a compromise. Europe would receive American arms, troops, and even a military leader, none other than General Dwight D. Eisenhower, in a new NATO military command. Supreme Headquarters Allied Powers Europe (SHAPE) under Supreme Allied Commander Eisenhower (who was also chief of the United States European Command) was a major confidence-builder. In return the anxious French, who could not accept an independent German force, agreed to lead a European army, in which German units would be placed under French leadership. The Pleven Plan of October 1950 would have Germans enter at the battalion level. This was raised to regimental level, as long as Germany would never exceed 20 percent of the total force. The result in the following year was the creation of a European Defense Community (EDC) which existed from May 1952 until August 1954.

American leaders were suspicious from the beginning that France had put forth the idea of a European army and community as a way of putting off American pressure, while receiving the benefits of 4 U.S. divisions and continued military aid. The American commitment was firm; the French response was filled with caveats. While most European allies agreed with France's suspicions of German reliability, the other partners in the European Defense Community recognized the absence of a credible alternative to a German contribution to NATO.

Only France was not satisfied, and proceeded to demand protocols binding as closely as possible the United States and Britain to the community. And still France failed to accept its own creation. The result was an American backlash against the French. A U.S. Senate vote of 88 to 0 on 31 July 1954 urged the president to give the Federal Republic full sovereignty, and perhaps even make a bilateral military alliance with West Germany if the French did not ratify the EDC treaty.

The initial disarray in the alliance resulting from France's action initially was quickly followed by imaginative proposals from Britain to bring Germany into NATO through an expanded Western Union, the progenitor of NATO. In the London and Paris agreements of September and October 1954, the European allies hammered out a plan whereby the West Germans would enter the alliance through membership in the Western Union, enlarged to include Italy as well, under the new name of Western European Union (WEU). France accepted Germany as a NATO ally when it would not be a partner in the defense community. The answer lay in part on French concern with loss of national identity in a "European" army, but moreso in the special terms whereby the WEU would restrict German manufacture of nuclear, biological, and chemical weaponry, as well as of warships and strategic bombers. While there would be German rearmament, which indeed was a key factor in the admission of the Federal Republic, its army would be wholly dedicated to the SHAPE command.

Although most of the restraints on German membership were quietly shelved over the next generation, the terms of West Germany's membership in 1955 disclose a unique way of enlarging the alliance. Spain's entry into NATO in 1982 as the sixteenth member offers still another model.

Spain (1982). Spain had been an unofficial associate of NATO long before it joined the alliance. Its geographic position on the western approach to the Mediterranean was a logical complement to Turkey's position on the eastern flank of the Mediterranean, and the strong anti-Communist posture of its leader, Generalissimo Francisco Franco, gave support to the major objective of the alliance in the Cold War. The fact of dictatorship itself did not bar Spain before 1982; Salazar's Portugal was no more democratic than its Iberian neighbor, and Greece under the colonels in the 1970s was hardly a model of democratic governance. But Franco's fascism in support of Hitler's Germany was a burden that kept the nation out of the alliance for a generation. Only Portugal lobbied for Spain's inclusion in 1949.

But once SHAPE came into being, the need for air and naval bases in Spain outweighed the obloquy of its fascist history, at least in the United States. From 1953 to Franco's death in 1976, the United States enjoyed Spanish base rights in return for economic and political support. While Spain's concessions were not enough to permit entry into NATO, their service to the defense of Europe was sufficient to allow NATO partners to accept Spain in the United Nations in 1956. But the price of the informal Franco-NATO ties and the close military connections with the United States was Spanish popular opposition to both the United States and NATO which erupted openly after Franco's death. The link between the dictator, Franco, and NATO reinforced an isolationism from the rest of

Europe which had been an important part of Spain's history. The continuing British control of Gibraltar was another barrier to post-Franco Spain's interest in joining the alliance.

With strong American backing, however, Spain's centrist government pressed for membership. By the end of the 1970s Western European governments were ready to accept democratic Spain into the alliance. The main opposition came from the powerful Socialist party which assumed power in October 1982, four months after Spain joined the alliance. Surprisingly, the youthful Socialist Premier, Felipe Gonzalez, whose platform promised a referendum which presumably would remove Spain from NATO, changed his mind about the connection, and carried the country with him. Fears of the security of Spanish enclaves in North Africa combined with a recognition that the Socialist governments of France and Italy would help Spain contain potential anti-democratic coups d'etat won support for NATO in the 1986 referendum.

The referendum also underscored Spain's refusal to integrate its forces into the military structure of NATO; it would be a member of the alliance, but not of the organization, in a manner similar to that of France, although for dissimilar reasons. Spain's interest in NATO in the 1980s was not stimulated by the Soviet threat but by the strength adherence would give to Spanish democracy and by the opportunity it might open for entry into the European Economic Community (EEC).

Partnership for Peace (1994). If the Partnership for Peace program should bring new nations into the alliance, it could cite a variety of precedents for admission to an "Atlantic" alliance which in 1995 was still dedicated to the security and stability of Europe. Spain provides a case study of an informal relationship in its pre-NATO experience, as well as an example of membership in the alliance but not in the organization. While France may be returning to the SHAPE-fold in the future, it is unlikely that Iceland, another member outside the organization, would change its status.

If concern about antagonizing and undermining the fragile Russian democracy becomes a paramount factor in preventing membership of former Warsaw Pact nations, possibilities of allaying Russian concerns may lie in affording the protection of the North Atlantic Treaty's Article 5 to Central and East European partners without a SHAPE-military presence beyond the German border. It may be worth noting that in the negotiations over the unification of Germany, the Soviet acceptance of East Germany into NATO was matched by West Germany's agreement to hold back a

NATO military presence in the former German Democratic Republic until Russian troops had evacuated the territory in 1994.

NATO's 46-year history not only shows no barriers to its enlargement, but also makes clear the pragmatic bases for membership. From the alliance's inception in 1949 the criteria had been the contributions the applicant would make to the security of the West in the broadest sense. Specific service to the containment of the Communist bloc was evident in such cases as Turkey and Germany. Protection of sea and air routes for American military assistance explains the presence of Iceland and Scandinavia in 1949. Prevention of Communist control by means of force as Norway feared, or by election as seemed possible in Italy in 1948, were major considerations. They carried more weight than the democratic credentials of a potential member. Yet the democratization as well as the security of Europe was always an objective, and membership in NATO fostered the growth of democracy in the Iberia peninsula after the passing of the dictators. The naming of the "North Atlantic Treaty" was designed to assure the allegiance of the North American partners in 1949, and from the beginning was open to loose construction.

Endnotes

1.   Partnership For Peace: Invitation Issued by Heads of State and Government Participating in the Meeting of the North Atlantic Council Held at NATO Headquarters, Brussels, January 10-11, 1994, *NATO Review*, Vol. 42 (February 1994), pp. 28-30.

2.   David Calleo, *The Atlantic Fantasy: The U.S., NATO, and Europe* (Baltimore: Johns Hopkins University Press, 1970), pp. 27-28; Geir Lundestad, "Empire By Invitation? The United States and Western Europe, 1945-1952," The Society for Historians of American Foreign Relations *Newsletter*, 15 (September 1984), pp. 1-21.

3.   Minutes, Fifth Meeting, Exploratory Talks, July 9, 1948, *Foreign Pelations of the United States (FRUS)*, 1948, 3:171.

4.   Sir Oliver Harvey to Bevin, March 2, 1949, FO 371/79231 8710/72G, Public Record Office, London.

5.   Acheson memorandum for Truman, April 8, 1949, *FRUS*, 1949, 3:176.

6.   North Atlantic Treaty, *Hearings*, before the Committee on Foreign Relations, U.S. Senate, 81 Congress, 1st Session, May 2, 1949, 1:282.

7.   Ibid., 2:341

8.   The Vandenberg Resolution and the North Atlantic Treaty, *Hearings*, held in executive session before the Committee on Foreign Relations, U.S. Senate, 81 Congress, 1st Session, on Executive Level, June 23, 1949, pp. 271-272.

9.   North Atlantic Treaty, *Hearings*, April 29, 1949, 1:281.

10. Ibid., April 27, 1949, 1:61.

11. To Amend the Mutual Defense Assistance Act of 1949, *Hearings*, U.S. Congress, House Committee on Foreign Relations, 81 Congress, 2nd Session, June 1950, p. 22.

12. "United States Interests, Positions, and Tactics at Paris," November 5, 1949, *FRUS*, 3:295.

MR. JEAN FÉLIX-PAGANON

Mr. Félix-Paganon is Political Director, Western European Union in Brussels. Prior to his current assignment, he was First Counsellor in the French Permanent Mission to the United Nations (New York). From 1989 to 1990, he was Diplomatic Advisor to the Ministry of Defence, Minister's Private Office in Paris. Other assignments include Deputy Director for the Middle East, Central Government (Paris) 1988-1989, Deputy Permanent Representative, French Delegation to the CSCE (Vienna) 1986-1988, Deputy Permanent Representative, French Delegation to the Conference on Disarmament in Europe (Stockholm) 1985-1986, and First Secretary, French Delegation to NATO (Brussels) 1983-1985. Mr. Felix-Paganon is a Graduate of the Paris Institut d'Études Politiques and the Institut national des Langues et Civilisations Orientales.

The Western European Union Path
2

Jean Félix-Paganon

The end of the Cold War and the collapse of the Soviet Union have led the member-states of the Atlantic Alliance, the European Union (EU) and Western European Union (WEU) fundamentally to reexamine how these organizations can contribute to enhancing security and stability on the European continent. This ongoing reexamination is addressing not only the roles these organizations should play in the new European security architecture, but also who should belong to them. Indeed these two aspects—missions and membership—are closely linked. It is therefore important to describe the development of the WEU's role in recent years, before addressing questions such as the relationship of the WEU's enlargement to that of the EU and NATO.

Role of Western European Union

Based on the Brussels Treaty of 1948 and modified by the Paris Agreements in 1954, the WEU was reactivated as an organization in the mid-1980s since it offered the only framework for wide-ranging consultations and cooperation between European Governments on security and defense questions. The Platform on European Security Interests, published in 1987, was the first concrete result of the early period of reactivation and was the first time since the Second World War that European Governments worked together to define their security interests and to further cooperation in defense matters. During the same period, both in the Iran-Iraq war and in the Gulf war, European Governments came together in the WEU framework to establish European naval coordination (minesweeping and embargo enforcement) in these international military operations. These actions helped to gain U.S. understanding and support for the emerging European security and defense identity.

These two aspects—policy consultations and operational cooperation—remain the two pillars of WEU activities. They were confirmed as such by the December 1991 Maastricht decisions which defined the WEU's role and its relations with the European Union and the Atlantic Alliance. As the Treaty on European Union states, "The common foreign and security policy shall include all questions related to the security of the Union, including the eventual framing of a common defense policy which might in time lead to a common defense."

However, for the time being the European Union recognized that defense matters must be taken forward in the WEU: "The Union requests the Western European Union, which is an integral part of the development of the Union, to elaborate and implement decisions and actions which have defense implications."

At the same time in Maastricht, the nine WEU member-states' Declaration defined the Organization's dual vocation—that the "WEU will be developed as the defense component of the European Union and as the means to strengthen the European pillar of the Atlantic Alliance." This declaration also committed the WEU member-states to strengthen the WEU's operational role.

To reflect the WEU's dual vocation, the WEU agreed to a separate Declaration on WEU enlargement offering full membership, or an observer status if they so wished, to the other European Union members and associate membership to the other European-NATO states not members of the European Union. As a result, Greece chose to become a full member, Denmark and Ireland observers, and Iceland, Norway, and Turkey took up the offer of associate membership. Following their accession to the European Union in January 1995, Austria, Finland, and Sweden also now sit at the WEU table as observers.

In the Petersberg Declaration of June 1992, the WEU's operational role was strengthened. Apart from contributing to the common defense, WEU military units could carry out the following missions:

- humanitarian and rescue tasks
- peacekeeping tasks
- crisis management, including combat forces in peacemaking.

The Petersberg Declaration also agreed that the WEU could provide missions in support of UN or Council on Security and Cooperation in Europe/Organization of Security and Cooperation in Europe (CSCE/OSCE) conflict prevention and crisis management activities. A Planning Cell was established to prepare the necessary planning for these types of missions and to maintain lists of the national and multinational units which WEU countries would be prepared to make available for WEU operations. The following multinational units have already been nominated: the EUROCORPS consisting of forces from France, Germany, Spain, Belgium and Luxembourg which will became operational at the end of 1995; the UK-Netherlands Amphibious Force; and the Belgian, German, Netherlands, and UK Multinational Division Central.

Much work has been undertaken over the past three years in implementing these decisions. Indeed, the forthcoming WEU Ministerial meeting in Lisbon will adopt a number of practical, but very important measures to improve WEU's political-military structures and the decision-making process.

The January 1994 Brussels Summit of NATO Heads of States and Governments was extremely important for WEU's development both politically and militarily. Politically, the Summit Declaration not only stressed the importance that all allies attach to the transatlantic link and to NATO's essential contribution to European security and stability, but also, through its reference to the language of Article J4 of the Treaty on European Union, all allies *including the United States* have given their support to the perspective of a European defense compatible with that of the Alliance. NATO's leaders acknowledged that a stronger European defense role—through the further development of the WEU—would reinforce the transatlantic link and enable the Europeans to take more responsibility for their common security and defense. Militarily, the Summit was important because the Alliance stressed its readiness to make its collective assets available for WEU operations. In particular, the concept of Combined Joint Task Forces (CJTF) was to be developed and implemented so as to allow for their employment by NATO or WEU.

WEU work on CJTFs has been proceeding. The WEU has developed criteria and modalities for the use of CJTFs. And this, together with the provisional assessment made by NATO of the WEU's paper, will now provide both organizations with a basis for moving forward. Clearly, many political and military obstacles still need to be overcome. However, the main objective must be to make European military structures sufficiently flexible and responsive so as to be able to undertake the highly varied missions likely to arise in the future, with different organizations (UN, OSCE, NATO, WEU) and participating countries. This must, of course, be done in a way which does not adversely affect the ability of the

Alliance to fulfill its fundamental task of the collective defense.

In recent years the WEU also played a part in projecting stability to the countries of Central and Eastern Europe. It established a Forum of Consultation in 1992 with, at the time, eight Central European countries; and in 1994 it agreed to a status of association with Bulgaria, the Czech Republic, Estonia, Hungary, Latvia, Lithuania, Poland, Romania, and Slovakia who became Associate Partners in WEU. The principal rationale for establishing this relationship with these nine Central European countries was that they sought membership in the European Union, notably through the Europe Agreements. The status of association enables the nine Associate Partners to contribute to WEU's discussions on European security and defense matters and offers them the possibility to participate in WEU "Petersberg-type" operations.

Following the mandate given by Ministers at the November 1994 meeting, all 27 WEU countries—full members, associate members, associate partners, and observers—are now participating in a "common reflection on the new European security conditions," which could lead to a French-proposed White Paper on European security. This is an important exercise, since it gathers around the same table all EU members, all European-NATO members, as well as countries which desire EU membership. The first part of the exercise, which should be completed by the Lisbon Ministerial meeting in May 1995, is a joint analysis of the European security environment and of the common security interests of the participating countries. The second part, to be undertaken in the second half of 1995, will aim to reach agreement on some appropriate responses. WEU countries have stressed the importance of ensuring that the exercise is "transparent" to the transatlantic allies and other European countries.

In addition, the WEU has also continued to develop the conceptual side of its activities. At the last Ministerial meeting of Noordwijk, the WEU agreed to "Preliminary Conclusions on a Common European Defense Policy." These conclusions summarize some of the WEU advances made in recent years and provide some guidelines for the future.

On the operational side, the WEU has been conducting three missions in former Yugoslavia. Although of a modest nature, given the challenges faced by the international community in former Yugoslavia, they are nevertheless functioning effectively and also reflect the three dimensions of WEU:

1) Operation SHARP GUARD to enforce the embargo in the Adriatic is conducted in conjunction with NATO;
2) the WEU is contributing a police contingent to the *European Union's* administration of the city of Mostar; and
3) the WEU has also established a mission on the Danube to support Bulgaria, Hungary, and Romania—three of WEU's *Associate Partners*—in enforcing sanctions there.

The Prospects for WEU, EU, and NATO Enlargement

Although much remains to be done, the WEU has made significant progress since Maastricht in its development as the defense component of the European Union and as the means to strengthening the European Alliance, in strengthening of its operational role and in contributing to stability in Europe more widely.

The prospects for the WEU's further enlargement are now, however, partially dependent on developments in other organizations. The WEU has now effectively put into place various sets of relationships which not only reflect WEU's role, but also the current, transitional phase in Europe's development. The WEU has 10 full member-states as its "hard core;" members both of the EU and of NATO, who, alone, have decision-making rights and have the responsibility to give the necessary political impetus to the organization.

To this hard core are associated the other EU members (of which all but one are not NATO members), the other non-EU European- NATO countries, and the prospective EU members from Central Europe. In addition to meetings of full members, the WEU Council meets "at 18" (members, observers, and associate members) to discuss matters particularly relating to the WEU's relations with the European Union and NATO and "at 27" for broader issues where the interests of WEU's Associate Partners are at stake.

Associate Members and Associate Partners may also participate in "Petersberg-type" missions, thereby offering WEU the opportunity to draw on a wider range of military forces. Finally, the arrival of the three new WEU observers—Austria, Finland, and Sweden—has raised the question of their possible role in WEU operational activities in the light of their extensive experience in peacekeeping. This system of "variable geometry" thus takes account of the differing memberships of the EU and

NATO and allows the WEU to develop its operational role to the maximum extent possible given the current security situation in which the 27 WEU countries find themselves.

The EU, for its part, has agreed that its next phase of enlargement, which would include certain Central European countries as well as Cyprus and Malta, should begin *only* after the Intergovernmental Conference (IGC) in 1996. At the IGC, the EU will face the issue of how to adapt its functions to cope with the prospect of a Union enlarged to 27 or more countries over the coming years. The IGC will also address the relationship between the EU's Common Foreign and Security Policy and WEU.

In parallel, the WEU will conduct its own review of its functions and relations with the EU and NATO. While WEU discussions have yet to begin, two considerations are likely to be of particular importance in preparation of this review. First, the fundamental decisions regarding defense and security will continue to be made on an intergovernmental basis. It is at present inconceivable that decisions such as the deployment of forces in international operations could be taken other than by national governments. Second, the solid relationship built through the years between the WEU and NATO will continue to be an important characteristic of post-IGC defense arrangements in Europe.

The principles of transparency, complementarity, and compatibility retain all their relevance. In particular, there is a clear recognition that disparities in the coverage provided by the respective defense commitments in the WEU and NATO Treaties should be avoided. Given these two considerations, the WEU seems well-placed to continue the development of a European security and defense identity.

The question of enlargement is of course most topical with regard to NATO in the light of the reaffirmation by Alliance leaders at the January 1994 summit: "Alliance . . . remains open to membership of other European States in a position to further the principles of the Treaty and to contribute to the security of the North Atlantic area." All aspects of this carefully drafted sentence need to be borne in mind when considering the enlargement of NATO. The extension of security guarantees is not to be taken lightly since such decisions affect stability in Europe as a whole and will be subject to ratification by all 16 existing member-states. In this regard, four considerations, which concern the relationships between the expansion of the WEU, EU, and NATO, need to be noted:

First, in the post Cold War world all three organizations have similar objectives: to enhance stability in Europe as a whole, and to create a security environment in which the countries of Central and Eastern Europe can accomplish their reform processes and further their economic and political development. Enlarging the EU, WEU, and NATO to Central Europe would be an essential means to this end.

Second, enlargement must not, however, alter the fundamental aims of the three organizations nor make their decision-making less effective.

Third, the manner and speed of the enlargement process must increase stability in the whole of Europe. The promotion of security and stability in Europe should be based on a comprehensive concept covering political, economic, and military aspects. All the organizations in Europe, as well as bilateral state relations, have complementary roles to play. For example, the OSCE has a crucial task as the only organization grouping the countries of North America, the whole of Europe and all of the former Soviet Union. It has established a set of principles by which the behavior of its members can be judged and its conflict prevention mechanisms can contribute to the peaceful settlement of disputes. Likewise, the Council of Europe has an important role to play, particularly in the area of human rights by strengthening relationships with those countries not included in the enlargement process. The European Union is developing multifaceted, political and economic relations with Russia and Ukraine. NATO's future relationship with Russia will be a key element in ensuring the future stability of Europe. The WEU, for its part, has also been enhancing exchanges of information and developing a dialogue with Russia and Ukraine in matters of mutual interest.

Fourth, it is important to bear in mind that the enlargement of the WEU, EU, and NATO are three independent processes which must take into account the different requirements of each organization and the different situations of potential candidate countries. We will therefore have to adopt a flexible approach.

Nevertheless, the view is widespread that, in the long run, the European memberships of the three organizations should converge. For the EU and WEU, WEU's Maastricht Declaration has already pointed in this direction. Equally, concerning WEU and NATO, there is a clear recognition that the creation of zones of different security by introducing disparities in the coverage provided by the respective defense commitments of the WEU and NATO should be avoided.

To summarize, the strength of the transatlantic link and the dynamic development of European integration enabled Western Europe to recover from the ravages of the Second World War. Now, in the post-Cold War era, the essential tasks facing all our countries is to manage the process while retaining the fundamental attributes of the system which has served us so well over the past 45 years while adapting and extending it principally to Central and Eastern Europe. This is a complex task not only given the overall international environment, but also because of severe restrictions on public expenditure we will need to explain effectively to our legislators and publics the objectives we are trying to achieve.

DR. JEFFREY SIMON

Dr. Simon is a Senior Fellow in the Institute for National Strategic Studies, National Defense University. Previously he was Chief, National Military Strategy Branch and Soviet Threat Analyst at the Strategic Studies Institute, U.S. Army War College. He has taught at Georgetown University and has held research positions at the System Planning Corporation, the RAND Corporation, and the American Enterprise Institute. Dr. Simon holds a Ph.D. from the University of Washington and an M.A. from the University of Chicago.

The PFP Path and Civil-Military Relations
3

Jeffrey Simon

The Central European revolutions of 1989 have been truly of historic proportions. They have not only captured the attention and imagination of the world, but have tested and challenged five states in the extreme—Germany, Poland, Hungary, and Czechoslovakia (now the Czech Republic and Slovakia).

The continuing transformations are much more encompassing and complex than the mere disintegration of communism. The aftershocks of World War I, which saw the disintegration of the Ottoman, Austro-Hungarian, and Russian empires, continue to haunt Central European successor states. Not only do the 1989-90 Central European revolutions have to deal with historically unfinished business,[1] they also test prevailing assumptions about civil-military relations in contemporary liberal democratic polities. And most important, the revolutions are likely to provide serious future challenges to U.S. and European security. History has been in fast-forward over the past five years. Already four distinct periods have been evident since the Central European revolutions of 1989-90. The present period is the one that may prove to be the most critical for Central Europe's future.

The first geo-strategic shift, which occurred during 1989-90, was marked by Central European euphoria resulting from the revolutions themselves, optimism about a "Return to Europe" by joining NATO and the European Community (EC)—now European Union (EU). The period witnessed NATO's July 1990 London Declaration extending a "hand of friendship" to the East. The period concluded with the successful Four-plus-Two (plus-One) negotiations culminating not only in Germany's October 3, 1990 unification, but also in NATO's enlargement to the Polish border to now incorporate the former German Democratic Republic in its security guarantee.

The second period, which occurred from German unification through the end of 1991, witnessed the disintegration of the Warsaw Pact, withdrawal of Soviet Groups of Forces from Hungary and Czechoslovakia, and a failed coup in the Soviet Union. During 1991 NATO convened ministerial meetings in Copenhagen (June), which sanctioned developing military ties to the east, and in Rome (November), which resulted in a new strategic concept (to replace NATO's Flexible Response) and the creation of the North Atlantic Cooperation Council (NACC) to engage the East. Central Europe's initial euphoria about West Europe's embrace of their "return" turned to more cautious (or realistic) optimism.

State disintegration marked the third period which opened in January 1992 and continued through 1993. The year 1992 witnessed the disintegration of the Soviet Union, former Yugoslavia, and Czechoslovakia marking the emergence of more than twenty new states. It also witnessed the continued withdrawal of Soviet (now Russian) troops from Germany and Poland in Central Europe.

NATO demonstrated willingness to engage in peacekeeping operations under either CSCE—Council on Security and Cooperation in Europe (May) or UN (December) auspices; and in June 1993, the NACC expressed its willingness to support the Alliance in UN and/or CSCE-mandated peacekeeping operations. The same period also witnessed Boris Yeltsin's initial support for, and change of mind about NATO's enlargement to Central Europe. NATO and EU hesitancy toward Central Europe coupled with Russia's pursuit of a Near Abroad policy and (again) failed coup in 1993 contributed to increasing Central European pessimism about Russia's prospects for democratic political development, security to the East, and skepticism about support from the West.

The fourth period opened with NATO's January 1994 Brussels Summit, which adopted the Combined Joint Task Force (CJTF), Partnership For Peace (PFP), and committed the Alliance to future expansion. During this period, the last of the Russian troops were withdrawn from Germany and Poland.

Central (and East Europeans), who were initially skeptical, if not cynical about Western intentions because they perceived the Alliance as bending to Russian opposition to their entry in 1993, have decided to test NATO in order to determine whether PFP and CJTF offer a real step toward NATO membership. In this regard, and with little doubt, the January 1994 Summit marked a watershed for NATO, but only time will tell whether the future Alliance will prove to be "hollow" or remain relevant to Europe's eastern security problems.

What NATO Has Done

NATO's responses to developments in the east—first, to the former Warsaw Pact members of Central and Eastern Europe, and second, to the new states emerging from the disintegrated Soviet Union—have been both extraordinary and insufficient. NATO's institutional responses have been extraordinary in that so many new initiatives have been taken in such a short period of time. Yet they have been insufficient in that events have moved at such a fast pace that NATO's responses have not kept up with expectations in the region.

London Declaration, July 1990. Only months after the revolutions of November-December 1989, NATO extended its first "hand of friendship" at the London Summit July 5-6, 1990. NATO invited the six (now former) Warsaw Pact members (Poland, Czechoslovakia, Hungary, Bulgaria, Romania and the Soviet Union) to visit Brussels to address the North Atlantic Council (NAC) and invited these governments to establish regular diplomatic liaison with NATO to share thinking and deliberations and to intensify military contacts during the period of historic change.[2] During the summer, new liaison ambassadors from the Warsaw Pact participated in briefings at NATO headquarters.

East German Absorption. East Germany's transformation from a key Warsaw Pact member in November 1989 to a full member of NATO on October 3, 1990 was unexpected and rapid. The Soviet position underwent unforeseen and mercurial twists on the security framework for a united Germany. Mikhail Gorbachev initially refused to accept the Germany-in-NATO framework when he met with George Bush on June 3, 1990. Though Gorbachev wanted a neutral unified Germany, his concession to Helmut Kohl in July indicated that he really had little choice in the matter. In reality, the Soviets ceded control when the former German Democratic Republic (GDR) failed to stabilize the domestic situation as a reform communist state in November 1989; *de facto* unification had occurred on July 1, 1990 with economic and monetary union of the two German states. The Soviets also decoupled political unification from the security issue when they conceded that all-German elections could occur irrespective of the Four-plus-Two agreement, which was signed on September 12, 1990.[3]

When formal unification occurred on October 3, 1990, Germany's five new eastern Laender (states formed from the former GDR) assumed

the protection of NATO's Article 5—"An armed attack against one . . .
shall be considered an attack against them all". NATO's enlargement east
occurred without the need to sign a new protocol of association as
employed upon the accessions of Greece and Turkey in 1951, Germany in
1955, and Spain in 1982.

Copenhagen NAC, June 1991. On June 6-7 NATO took the next step
at the Copenhagen NAC session by agreeing to implement a broad set of
further initiatives "to intensify . . . [NATO's] program of military contacts
at various levels"[4] with Central and East European (CEE) states. CEE
military contacts would be intensified with NATO headquarters, SHAPE,
and other major NATO commands, and NATO would invite CEE military
officers to NATO training facilities for special programs concerning civilian oversight of defense. Meetings of experts would be held to discuss
security policy issues, military strategy and doctrine, arms control, and
military industrial conversion to civilian purposes. NATO invited CEE
experts to participate in NATO's "Third Dimension" scientific and envi-
ronmental programs and to exchange views on subjects such as air space
management. Also NATO information programs expanded to the CEE
region.

NAC Ministerial, August 21, 1991. Until August, NATO treated all
former Warsaw Pact countries alike. During the August 1991 coup
attempt in the then-Soviet Union, the August 21 NAC ministerial statement differentiated the Soviet Union from the other Warsaw Pact countries, when it suspended liaison "pending a clarification in that country."
The statement also noted:

> We expect the Soviet Union to respect the integrity and security
> of all states in Europe. As a token of solidarity with the new
> democracies of Central and Eastern Europe, we will develop
> ways of further strengthening our contribution toward the politi-
> cal and economic reform process within these countries. Our
> diplomatic liaison arrangements with the Central and eastern
> European democracies now take on added significance.[5]

**Rome Summit, November 1991: Genesis of NATO's Political and
Military Transformation.** At the November 7-8, 1991 Rome NAC summit, NATO approved the Rome Declaration which broadened NATO's
activities with the Soviet Union and Central and East Europe to include

annual meetings with the NAC at ministerial level in what would be called the North Atlantic Cooperation Council (NACC); periodic meetings with the NAC at ambassadorial level; additional meetings as circumstances warrant; and regular meetings with NATO subordinate committees, including the Political and Economic Committees; and the Military Committee and other NATO military authorities.[6] In addition to creating the NACC, the November 1991 Rome summit initiated another major change when it adopted a New Strategic Concept to replace its 1967 strategy of "Flexible Response." The new strategy moved NATO's military emphasis away from massive mobilization toward enhanced crisis management capabilities and peacekeeping operations. It also established the groundwork for NATO's military transformation.

North Atlantic Cooperation Council (NACC).[7] On December 20, 1991 the foreign ministers of all the "former adversaries" (including the newly independent Latvia, Lithuania, and Estonia) met at the inaugural NACC to adopt a "Statement on Dialogue, Partnership, and Cooperation" that endorsed annual meetings of the NACC at ministerial level; bimonthly meetings of the NAC with liaison ambassadors beginning February 1992; additional NACC meetings as circumstances warrant; and regular meetings of the Political, Economic, and Military Committees with liaison partners. The purpose of the consultations and cooperation would be on security and related issues.

On February 26, the NACC met at the ambassadorial level to discuss and adopt a "Work Plan for Dialogue, Partnership, and Cooperation." The March 10, 1992 Extraordinary NACC meeting, which convened to broaden membership to 35 (to include the former Soviet republics except Georgia), endorsed the Work Plan, which covered a wide set of activities including defense planning issues, defense conversion, economic issues, science, challenges of modern society, dissemination of information, policy planning consultations, and air traffic management.[8]

While the NACC had laudable goals and its activities have mushroomed, its limitations immediately became apparent. First, the disintegration of the Soviet Union at the end of 1991 and the decision to include all its successor states as new NACC members meant that rather than the originally conceived five non-Soviet Warsaw Pact members and the USSR, the NACC would include more than twenty new members. The immense diversity among NACC partners (e.g., between Poland and Uzbekistan) led to Central European demands for differentiation and increasing demands for membership in the Alliance. In sum, despite well-intended goals, the cooperation partner's demands on the NACC made it quite apparent how ill-prepared and limited the organization really was. NATO's recognition of its inadequacy came in January 1994 when in lieu of extending membership, the North Atlantic Council adopted the Partnership For Peace (PFP) program.

NATO and NACC as "Out-Of-Area" Peacekeeper

Oslo NAC/NACC, June 1992. On June 4, 1992 the North Atlantic Council (NAC) Foreign Ministers session in Oslo agreed "to support on a case-by-case basis in accordance with their own procedures, peace-keeping activities under the responsibility of the CSCE."[9] Immediately afterward, NATO moved "out-of-area" and with the WEU dispatched naval units to the Adriatic to enforce the UN embargo. Many NACC members evidently saw this as an opportunity to broaden their coopera-tion with NATO and on June 5 the NACC foreign ministers attached "par-ticular importance to enhancing the CSCE's operational and institutional capacity to contribute to conflict prevention, crisis management, and the peaceful settlement of disputes [and expressed willingness] to con-tribute."[10]

In December 1992 the NATO NAC Ministerial extended a parallel offer to the UN; it noted the Alliance's readiness "to support peacekeep-ing operations under the authority of the UN Security Council."[11] The NACC then followed by agreeing that NATO and cooperation partners would share experience with one another and with other CSCE states in the planning and preparation of peacekeeping missions and would con-sider possible joint peacekeeping training and exercises. The same NACC also approved a 1993 Work Plan with specific provisions on peacekeep-ing and created a NACC Ad Hoc Group on Cooperation in Peacekeeping, to discuss general political and conceptual principles and practical mea-sures for cooperation.

Closer cooperation and confidence among NACC partners became evident in February 1993 when the Military Committee met for the first time in a cooperation session. When NACC defense ministers met at the end of March 1993, they recognized the importance "of the ability to act in a cooperative framework" in peacekeeping tasks and "ensure that a high priority be given this work."[12]

On April 12, 1993, under authority of UN Resolution 816, NATO started the no-fly zone enforcement-operation over Bosnia-Herzegovina. In late April, the Military Committee again met in cooperation with Chiefs of Defense Staff (CHODs) to discuss the possibility of NATO intervention in Bosnia should a peaceful solution fail.

Athens NAC/NACC, June 1993. The June 10, 1993 NAC ministerial communique noted the development of a "common understanding on conceptual approaches to peacekeeping [and] enhancing of cooperation in this field"[13] with Cooperation Partners. The June 11, 1993 Athens NACC adopted the Ad Hoc Group's detailed Report on Cooperation in Peacekeeping[14] and agreed to accelerate the Ad Hoc Group's practical cooperation to implement the program, including the sharing of experience in peacekeeping planning, training and exercises, and logistics.[15] As a result of the Athens NACC session, Prague hosted a high-level NACC seminar on peacekeeping from June 30 to July 2 to discuss conceptual and doctrinal issues of peacekeeping.[16]

In sum, it is evident that NATO has been quite responsive in a very short period of time. But has it been enough? The CEE countries clearly believe that more than meetings alone is necessary, if NATO is to serve an essential role in the protection of European peace and stability. Particularly as the NACC has broadened its membership so rapidly, it suffers the danger of becoming "neutralized" as a credible security institution. In concrete terms what will be NATO's and NACC's role in the event of a real crisis? These are the questions that are coming to the forefront particularly from the so-called Visegrad states—Poland, Hungary, Czech Republic, and Slovakia. All have expressed the desire for a differentiated role within NATO/NACC. They want criteria and time-lines to become full members of NATO and have agreed to accept responsibilities for NATO's security concerns.

NATO's January 1994 Brussels Summit: A Watershed. Although it took NATO twenty-four years to adopt a new Strategic Concept to replace its Flexible Response strategy in November 1991, one might argue that with Yugoslavia's and the Soviet Union's disintegration, Russia's recent efforts to reassert influence over the Commonwealth of Independent States (CIS), and resulting insecurities in Central Europe, that NATO now needs a "new" Strategic Concept.

Whether the January 1994 NATO Brussels Summit actually will prove to be a such a watershed remains to be seen. The Summit did attempt to fuse together the more flexible force structure packages for peacekeeping requirements (the so-called Combined Joint Task Force (CJTF)) with NATO's new need to stabilize the East by adopting the Partnership For Peace (PFP) plan.

In support of the development of a European Security and Defense Identity (ESDI) and the strengthening of the European pillar of the Alliance through the Western European Union (WEU), the Summit agreed that in future contingencies "NATO and the WEU will consult. . . through joint Council meetings [and] . . . stand ready to make collective assets of the Alliance available . . . for WEU operations."[17] As a result, the Summit endorsed the CJTF as a means to facilitate contingency operations, including peacekeeping operations with participating nations outside the Alliance.

Though the Summit did not accede to Central Europe's desire for immediate membership, the Partnership for Peace (PFP) proposal did establish NATO's long-term commitment to expand, leaving vague both the criteria and time-lines for expansion.[18] Operating under the authority of the NAC, active participation in PFP is seen as a necessary (though not sufficient) condition to joining NATO. Partner states will participate in political and military bodies at NATO headquarters and in a separate Partnership Coordination Cell (PCC) at Mons that will:

> work in concrete ways towards transparency in defense budgeting, promoting democratic control of defense ministries, joint planning, joint military exercises, and creating an ability to operate with NATO forces in such fields as peacekeeping, search and rescue and humanitarian operations . . . .[19]

While the goals of NATO's CJTF and PFP are explicit and can be seen as a hedging against possible future problems in the East, their implementation might have some more immediate, unwitting, and unwanted regional implications. If we are not careful, PFP could undermine:

1) Central East Europe's sub-regional cooperation by turning local actors into competitors;
2) domestic support for the region's democratic reformers;
3) the region's fragile civil-military relations; and

4) sub-regional security by attracting scarce defense resources from Central Europe's real defense requirements.

What Central Europe Has Done

Immediately after the January 10-11, 1994 NATO summit had initiated PFP and CJTF and announced that NATO was open to future expansion, President Clinton visited Prague (on January 12) to meet with the presidents of the four Central European (Visegrad) states to explain the program. In advance, the Central European defense ministers (except the Czech Republic, which sent First Deputy Defense Minister Jiri Pospisil) met in Warsaw to prepare for the forthcoming meeting with President Clinton. After the session, the defense ministers declared they expected the PFP program to open the way to permanent contacts with NATO and lead to full membership in the Alliance.[20]

Poland. Following a January 10, 1994 cabinet session, Polish Foreign Minister Andrzej Olechowski appraised PFP as "too small a step in the right direction" and President Walesa noted that NATO is committing a "serious error" in bowing to Russian objections. Walesa also harshly criticized the Czechs for failing to support a coordinated Visegrad strategy toward NATO.[21] Though Polish Defense Minister Kolodziejczyk added that he understood the West's difficulty to put forward a precise date for integration, he noted, "We expect NATO to come up with clear criteria in the short term for NATO membership."[22]

After the NATO summit, Walesa went to Prague for talks with the other Visegrad presidents and President Clinton (on January 12). Because the Czech Republic wanted the talks conducted on a bilateral basis, Walesa expressed anger with the Czech's course of action: "They are making a mistake that will cost us all something."[23] After the session with President Clinton, Foreign Minister Olechowski noted: "[W]e have many promises, political declarations, but we lack specific prospects."[24]

Though Poland had initially exhibited reserve, it responded rapidly. One of the immediate requirements of the Partnership for Peace program was the need to find funding. Kolodziejczyk estimated that the Army would need an additional 500 billion zlotys ($23 million) to participate. (The overall 1994 Polish defense budget was only 47.8 trillion zlotys ($4.2 billion) or 2.2 percent of GDP).[25] On February 2, 1994 Prime Minister Pawlak signed documents in Brussels making Poland the third nation to signify its intention to participate in PFP. However, unlike his Romanian and Lithuanian predecessors, Pawlak stated that Poland was not really happy with PFP, but "[W]e can accept it if we are certain that Poland will ultimately be able to become a full member."[26]

Despite its initial reservation, Poland's foreign and defense ministries in conjunction with Sejm committees on defense and foreign affairs worked out a response.[27] On April 25, 1994 Poland became the first partner to hand over a Presentation Document to NATO outlining the spheres of its intended cooperation with the Alliance. At the May 25, 1994 NATO and PFP defense ministers meeting in Brussels, Kolodziejczyk continued to voice concern that "something is lacking" that the program fails to define clearly how to move from partnership to membership.[28]

Then on July 5 Poland became the first partner to sign an Individual Partnership Program (IPP). In addition to peacekeeping missions and joint exercises, Poland incorporated additional amendments to its IPP to include air defense, convergence of command, control, and communications systems, and democratic control of the armed forces.[29] The 32-page document contained 60 specific measures covering training, exercises, and information exchanges which would cost Poland 250 billion zlotys for 1994.[30]

When President Clinton visited Warsaw and addressed the Polish Sejm on July 7, 1994, he noted that NATO expansion is "no longer a question of whether, but when and how."[31] Of the $100 million he pledged in U.S. support of the overall PFP program, Clinton committed $25 million to Poland.

Polish contacts with NATO began to mushroom. In mid-May 1994 a 96-soldier company from the British army began a small bilateral peace-keeping exercise with Polish troops at Kielce (Poland), that was billed as being "in the spirit of NATO's PFP plan."[32] The first real PFP ground forces exercise, "Cooperative Bridge-94" took place September 12-16 at Biedrusko near Poznan, Poland. Some 920 soldiers (of which 280 were Polish) from 13 countries were divided into five multi-national companies under Polish-American command.[33]

Polish military contacts with Germany also began to flourish, particularly after September 1, 1994 when the last Russian troops had departed Germany and Poland. The Bundeswehr sponsored special ties with Polish units and exercises in the Polish border region.[34] On September 1, General Naumann and Polish CoS Wilecki signed a partnership agreement for individual units of the two forces.[35] During 1994, the Polish, German, and French (so-called Weimar triangle) defense ministers also met often to discuss how to expand cooperation,[36] and German General Henning von Ondarza began to act as an adviser to the Polish defense minister.[37] Culminating the 1994 training year (September 16-23), Polish ground forces, a Danish mechanized platoon, and German air-landing company held a peacekeeping operation, "Tatra-94" in the Krakow Military District.[38]

Hungary. Though Partnership for Peace had only become an official NATO policy on January 10, 1994, Csaba Kiss of the Hungarian defense ministry noted (on January 13) that defense officials had been working on Hungary's plan since October 1993. Kiss noted that PFP would require Hungarian defense planning and spending to be more open and in line with NATO standards, and under more civilian control. He added that Hungarian soldiers would participate in future peacekeeping operations, that Hungary's air defense and airspace management needed to be converted to NATO formats (with IFF and ground radars overhauled to communicate with NATO aircraft), and that two military planners would go to Brussels.[39]

On February 8 Foreign Minister Geza Jeszenszky signed Hungary's PFP presentation document, making it the fifth state to join; and on November 15, 1994 Hungary submitted its Individual Partnership Program in Brussels.[40]

The Hungarian Parliament authorized holding a joint British-Hungarian PFP military exercise ("Hungarian Venture") from September 1-25, 1994 on Hungarian soil. The exercise involved 140 British troops and 228 Hungarian soldiers, including its peacekeeping company.[41] One lesson Hungary learned from the exercise was that differences in staff-level work and linguistic problems rather than incompatibility of weapons hampered cooperation.[42] Because of the shortage of funds, this was the only exercise Hungary held during 1994; Hungary did not participate in the first large-scale PFP exercise "Cooperative Bridge-94" in Poland.[43]

Hungary's fiscal constraints limited its participation. Defense Minister Keleti, regretting Hungary's inability to participate in PFP exercises in Poland and the Netherlands, noted the defense ministry would need 493 million forints for the individual tasks undertaken in PFP.[44] On November 16 the National Assembly Defense Committee approved the 1995 defense budget which would increase to 77.1 billion forints (up 8 billion from 1994).

Czech Republic. With NATO's introduction of Partnership For Peace (PFP), Defense Minister Antonin Baudys noted that all exercises undertaken by the Czech Army would be subject to the consent of parliament. On April 29, 1994, the Parliament approved the government proposal to permit short-term military training and exercises on Czech soil (5,000 foreign troops for up to 21 days) and for Czech units to participate abroad (700 troops for up to 30 days).[45]

On March 10, 1994 when Vaclav Klaus signed the PFP general agreement making the Czech Republic the 11th country to join the project, Defense Minister Baudys noted that the program "is the maximum possible and the minimum desired."[46] The Czech's first joint exercise under PFP on Czech soil took place March 15-25, 1994, when 32 Dutch marines participated with 120 troops of the Czech Rapid Deployment Battalion. Then during May 29-June 10, 130 French troops participated in exercises in the Czech Republic with 120 members of a company of the 23rd Czech Mechanized Battalion.[47] Again during September 9-19, a platoon of 40 soldiers of the Czech 4th mechanized regiment participated in "Cooperative Bridge-94."[48] Finally, the training year concluded with the first joint Czech-German military exercise of 400 troops, which took place during November 7-11, on both sides of the common border.[49]

The new Czech Defense Minister Wilem Holan noted, in reference to NATO membership, "It is possible to anticipate that the conditions for NATO membership will be clearly defined in the near future—that is, certain standards will be drawn up . . . [adding the warning that] the 'cheap' phase of our decisions is coming to an end, and the phase that will cost us something is beginning."[50]

Slovakia. The fundamental orientation of Slovakia is to obtain full NATO membership. The starting point for this objective is participating in NATO's NACC and Partnership For Peace (PFP). It signed its Presentation Document on May 25, 1994.[51] The ongoing process of building its defense ministry and armed forces from scratch led to a slow start and fiscal constraints have limited Slovakia's participation. The internal political struggle causing government instability also contributed to a *slower* start.

In addition to small group exchanges, Slovakia participated in "Cooperation Bridge-94" in Poland and in a military exercise in the Netherlands in October. Slovakia's first Defense Minister Imrich

Andrejcak criticized his successor's (Pavol Kanis) changes to the PFP presentation document as too expensive; Andrejcak argued that the defense ministry would be required to spend 4.5 percent of its budget on PFP, rather than the one percent originally envisaged.[52]

NATO Brussels Summit, December 1, 1994

When the NAC met in Brussels on December 1, 1994, 23 countries had so-far joined the Partnership (Belarus and Austria became the 24th and 25th in early 1995 and 10 IPP's had been signed), the Partnership Coordination Cell at Mons had become fully operational (11 Partners had already appointed liaison officers to the Cell), and three PFP exercises had been held in the Autumn of 1994.

The Brussels Summit communique reaffirmed that the Alliance:

remains open to membership . . . [and] expects and would welcome NATO enlargement that would reach to democratic states to our East. [Accordingly, they made a decision to begin an extensive study] to determine how NATO will enlarge, the principles to guide this process and the implications of membership.[53]

On December 2, 1994 the NACC foreign ministers convened (along with those members who had joined PFP but were not in NACC) and were informed about the NAC decision to initiate the study to determine the modalities for NATO expansion.[54] Thus informed, Hungarian Foreign Minister Kovacs responded that NATO expansion should be gradual, predictable, and transparent.[55]

The May 30, 1995 NAC Ministerial at Noordwijk, in the Netherlands noted "satisfaction with the progress in the internal study"[56] to determine how NATO will enlarge and agreed to present it to the Partners prior to the next NAC meeting in Brussels in December 1995.

Guidelines for expansion. While we do not know precisely what the Alliance will approve as necessary guidelines for expansion, it is likely that they will include: active participation in NACC and the PFP, the successful performance of democratic political institutions, a free market economy, and respect for human rights. It is also likely that effective democratic control of the military as well as some minimal degree of military capability and NATO interoperability will be necessary conditions.

NATO's challenge, though, will be how to define and determine what constitutes "effective" democratic control of the military recognizing that each state has its own history, culture, and unique set of institutions. The study posits the following four conditions as being necessary for "effective" civilian oversight of the military:

1) **A clear division of authority** between the president and government (prime minister and defense minister) in constitutions, amendments, or through public law. The law should clearly establish who commands and controls the military and promotes senior military officers in peacetime, who holds emergency powers in crisis, and who has authority for the transition to war.

2) **Parliamentary oversight** of the military through control of the defense budget. Its role in deploying armed forces in emergency and war must be clear.

3) **Peacetime government control** of general staffs and military commanders through civilian defense ministries. Control should include preparation of the defense budget, access to intelligence, involvement in strategic planning, force structure development, arms acquisitions and deployments, and military promotions.

4) **Restoration of military prestige, trustworthiness and accountability** for the armed forces to be effective. Having come from the communist period when the military was often used as an instrument of external or internal oppression, society must perceive the military as being under effective national control. Military training levels and equipment must also be sufficient to protect the state.

If NATO comes to define these four conditions as necessary for exercising "effective" democratic control of the military, most Central European (Visegrad) states—those frequently referred to as the most likely to first join NATO—would *not* meet these standards. When examining Central Europe's civil-military progress since the 1989 revolutions, it is clear that much has already been achieved. It is equally clear that much remains to be done!

What Needs to Be Done?

Poland. In the initial 1988-June 1989 phase of round-table discussions, Poland effectively wrested the National Defense Council (KOK), which controlled the defense and interior ministries, from the communist party placing it under de jure control of the newly-formed institution of president (communist party leader Jaruzelski became president). Since April 8, 1989 the KOK was no longer a supra-governmental agency, but a collegial state organ subordinate to Parliament. This was of immense importance because of Poland's historic experience with the defense council during the Marshal Jozef Pilsudski and 1980-81 martial law eras. In the second phase, after the June 1989 elections, Parliament began to exert greater moral authority (reformers now controlled the Senate; and the one-third of the Sejm) and some oversight of the military. Ad hoc Solidarity reformers and Parliament established oversight groups in the defense ministry. Two Solidarity civilians (Bronislaw Komorowski and Janusz Onyszkiewicz) became deputy defense ministers and began efforts to eliminate the Main Political Administration (communist party) from the military and control contact with foreign states and international institutions (in part, to ensure that the Soviet Union could no longer command Polish armed forces through the Statute system). Piotr Kolodziejczyk, an independent-minded admiral, became defense minister in July 1990; General Zdzsislaw Stelmaszuk, who never attended a Soviet staff college, became chief of staff (CoS). Because President Jaruzelski's moral prestige had greatly declined after the elections, he resigned and requested that new presidential elections be held two-and one-half years early.

The third phase began after Lech Walesa was elected president by popular mandate in December 1990. Power began to shift from Parliament (the Sejm still had two-thirds communist membership) to the president. Not only did Walesa now chair the KOK, which provided reformers with *de facto* control of the military and police, but Walesa exercised oversight by attempting to change the KOK to the National Security Council by taking it away from the defense ministry and putting it under presidential financial control. He also expanded his authority over the National Security Bureau (BBN), which developed Poland's military doctrine, developed threat analyses, and drafted the reforms to reorganize the defense ministry and restructure the General Staff. Poland's efforts to write a Constitution during this period were frustrated by tensions between the communist-dominated Sejm on the one hand, and the Senate and president on the other. Frustrated with the Sejm, Walesa pushed for parliamentary elections two-and-one-half years earlier than planned.

The October 1991 parliamentary elections marked the fourth phase. Though Poland's legislative and executive institutions were now fully legitimate in democratic political terms, a heavily fragmented and weak coalition government and the absence of a Constitution became its Achilles heel. Debates over a new Constitution brought tensions and political showdown between the Parliament (Sejm and Senate) and the president.

Ambiguity in authority and differences in interpretation over command and control of the military caused the downfall of Poland's first civilian Defense Minister Jan Parys, and then of Prime Minister Jan Olszewski and his government. When the Sejm Commission examined Parys' allegations that Walesa had been planning martial law contingencies and offered Silesian Military District commander Tadeusz Wilecki the position of Chief of Staff for his support, it exonerated the president. Defense Minister Onyszkiewicz (and Prime Minister Hanna Suchocka) initially brought new cooperation between the government and the president and some progress in defense ministry efforts to establish oversight of the military. On October 22, 1992 Onyszkiewicz implemented the inter-ministerial commission's reform of the defense ministry. The defense ministry now had three departments (strategy, training, and logistics) and military courts and intelligence were subordinated to the civilian defense minister. Though Onyszkiewicz attempted to fuse the civilian defense ministry financial and personnel services with the General Staff, and Deputy Defense Minister Jan Kuriata attempted set up an independent department to oversee military infrastructure and acquisition, these efforts were frustrated by the General Staff which had been restructured to correspond with the defense ministry's three departments.

But these defense ministry efforts were further limited by the fact that President Walesa *did* appoint General Wilecki to be chief of staff and Wilecki continued to arrogate power by bringing his military district commanders to the General Staff. In sum, the General Staff effectively maintained autonomy by playing off civilian defense ministry oversight against the president.

Though the so-called Small Constitution (November 1992) was a provisional effort to clarify legislative and executive authority and define president and government powers, it failed because of continued ambiguity. Lack of consensus was evident in the seven Constitutional drafts submitted to the Constitutional Commission, the Sejm Defense Committee's opposition to the president's oversight of a National Guard, and in differing views of the president's role in appointing ministers of defense, interior, and foreign affairs.

The fifth period began with the post-communist SDP-PPA coalition victory in the September 1993 Parliamentary elections. Once again, the absence of a Constitution contributed to lack of effective civilian oversight of the military and to governmental crisis and collapse. The defense ministry's reduced role was evident in Defense Minister Piotr Kolodziejczyk's early actions. In November 1993 he reduced the defense ministry staff and restructured the ministry by unifying the strategy and training directorates under a 1st deputy, Jerzy Milewski who retained his BBN position. He gave the General Staff more authority by transferring the civilian Department of Education back to the military, creating a fourth organization/mobilization directorate, and placing intelligence and counterintelligence under its purview. In the September 1994 Drawsko affair, when the president undermined the defense minister's authority, the military gained greater autonomy.

As a result of Drawsko, not only did the defense minister have to resign (contributing to the Pawlak government's ultimate collapse), but the Sejm Defense Committee's investigation commission also equivocated in its findings. Though the Sejm Committee criticized the president for his behavior at Drawsko, it failed to react even after the president presented awards to General Wilecki and other top military commanders after the incident. Walesa also continued to challenge the defense minister's list of general officers for promotion and the government's authority to appoint so-called "presidential ministers," causing the collapse of the Pawlak government. In effect, the government had lost effective control and oversight over the military.

Poland, has not yet fulfilled what are likely to be defined as necessary conditions for effective civilian control of the military and for NATO membership. Government crises and lack of effective civilian oversight of the military will continue until Poland has adopted a new Constitution that establishes clear lines of authority between president and government and returns enough authority to the civilian defense ministry to provide effective oversight of the military. Poland's civil-military crisis must be resolved because Polish society today holds the military in very high esteem, and because the military has traditionally been used for internal and external purposes. The absence of any clear command authority and of civilian control over the military is a recipe for disaster.

In sum, Poland has come a long way in restoring prestige to the military. Parliament has reassumed effective oversight of the defense budget, even if it did twice equivocate on whether the president or defense minister controls the military and fail to reform the law. Onyszkiewicz has begun to restructure the armed forces to be compatible with NATO. Though Kolodziejczyk continued this process and stemmed the defense budget slide (since 1986), the military still has a way to go to achieve NATO compatibility. So Poland's reform is yet incomplete.

Hungary. The October 1989 Constitution, which replaced Hungary's 1949 Constitution, was written by reform communists to establish authority between the president, government, and National Assembly, which only by majority could declare a state of emergency or war. Most importantly In February 1990, the Hungarian National Assembly claimed national control of the armed forces when it assumed the authority to deploy Hungarian forces at home and abroad. This power effectively terminated the Soviet Statute System in Hungary, which had provided the former USSR direct control of the Hungarian armed forces.

Reform communists promulgated a Defense Reform (December 1, 1989) that created many problems between presidential and governmental authority. The reform separated the armed forces from the defense minister and placed them under the president who the communists originally thought would be their reform leader Imre Poszgay. Thus, when Hungary became the first Central European state to appoint a civilian defense minister (Lajos Fur chairman of the MDF in May 1990), the Commander of the Hungarian Army was not subordinate to him, but to the president, who had authority to appoint and promote generals.

After the March 1990 elections, which resulted in a Free Democrat (AFD) president (Arpad Goncz) and Hungarian Democratic Forum (MDF) government (Jozsef Antall), the new Hungarian government had to undo the problems created by the December 1989 communist legacy. Indeed, most of Hungary's defense reform has involved amending the Constitution (e.g., In June 1990 it was amended to require a Parliamentary two-thirds rather than simple majority to employ armed forces) and/or testing it in the Constitutional Court.

Civil-military problems arose over the issues of control of professional military education and military institutes (defense minister or Army Commander), the use of the armed forces during domestic transport strikes (president or defense minister) and during Yugoslav air-space violations (Parliament or government). Differences became so tense, that Hungarian Commander Kalman Lorincz resigned in frustration and the government during 1991 sought Constitutional Court decisions on presidential and governmental authority over the Hungarian armed forces during peacetime and crisis.

The Court's decisions in favor of the government led to the 1992 Defense Reform that restructured the defense ministry so the defense minister could assume oversight of the armed forces, military intelligence, and recommend military promotions for presidential approval. During 1993 a Defense Law gave Fur the authority to fuse the positions of Hungarian Army Commander with the Chief of the General Staff, and on December 7, constitutional amendments placed the border guard under the police in peacetime (hence, under government control) and gave the government authority to call up to 5,000 troops in an emergency without specific agreement of the president or declaration by Parliament. Parliament retained authority to approve the principles of National Defense, military development, and the budget.

Though the Main Political Administration was eliminated from the armed forces, Defense Minister Fur packed the defense ministry with MDF civilians, creating a new form of political influence. This action created problems after the May 1994 elections that returned the post-communist Hungarian Socialist Party (HSP) in coalition with the AFD to power by two-thirds majority. Under the new government, the defense ministry was subordinated to retired colonel Gyorgy Keleti, who had been relieved by Fur as defense ministry spokesman. Keleti now replaced MDF civilians with retired or acting military officers, reorganized the defense ministry and reduced its staff, provided the General Staff more authority in military planning (to include intelligence), and reversed an earlier decision to separate the position of chief of staff from Hungarian Army Commander. Keleti's actions raise questions about "effective" civilian defense ministry oversight of the military.

Hungary also needs a new constitution, but Hungary's two-thirds Parliamentary majority may not be able to develop the broad-based consensus necessary for a constitution. Among other things, the constitution needs to clarify the role of the president during war (symbolic or real) and establish a new constitutional (presently two-thirds) amending formula.

On the military side, the armed forces have been significantly cut from 120,000 to 65,000 and are being restructured for NATO integration. But financial resources have greatly constrained Hungary's armed forces restructuring, modernization, and PFP-exercise participation.

To conclude, Parliament has been effective in exerting control of the defense budget and deploying Hungarian armed forces. The Constitutional Court's decisions have been respected and have led to major defense reforms allowing the government (prime minister and defense minister) to take control of the military in peacetime and emergency. However, Hungary still needs a constitution (that is not a two-thirds majority victor's mandate) to define the president's wartime powers. Also in light of recent defense ministry and General Staff changes, Hungary needs to reassert effective "civilian" defense ministry oversight of the military.

Czechoslovakia. Both Czech and Slovak successor states benefitted from three years of reform in Czechoslovakia. Czechoslovakia's revolution was swift. By the end of December 1989 the Federal Assembly had elected Vaclav Havel president. The fact that Havel wielded national command authority was particularly important for Czechoslovakia not only because of the Statute System, but also because its military, in contrast to Poland and Hungary, had been involved in failed efforts at counter-revolution in 1989 (Operation Wave).

By the end of 1989, the president (not the party secretary) chaired the Defense Council, General Vaclavik (who had given orders to prepare to use force in Operation Wave) was replaced by General Vacek as defense minister, and a Civic Forum civilian, Antonin Rasek, became deputy defense minister. During 1990 Parliament created an Inspector General to oversee the defense ministry and various Civic Forum and government oversight bodies were attached to the armed forces to screen military cadres and monitor democratization. After a Commission concluded that Vacek had been involved in Operation Wave, Lubos Dobrovsky became Czechoslovakia's first civilian defense minister in October.

When Dobrovsky took over, he demanded another screening of cadres and he assumed control of (military and interior) intelligence and counterintelligence. During the spring of 1991 the defense ministry was restructured into three directorates (strategy, economics, and social and human affairs) to strengthen civilian oversight, and Karel Pezl, who had been cashiered from the armed forces in 1968 and was now deemed politically reliable, became chief of staff of the armed forces. Widespread screening of senior officers then ensued. Elections in June 1992 sealed the disintegration of the federation. During the last half of 1992, Czech and Slovak attention turned to preparing new constitutions and planning to divide their armed forces and property. While both successor states had the benefit of three years of Czechoslovak defense reform, each faced different problems as 1993 began.

Czech Republic. The Czech Republic has enjoyed political stability and has accomplished much in the area of defense reform since independence. The defense ministry appears to have established "effective" control of the military. Antonin Baudys, a civilian, became the first Czech defense minister. He initially retained Karel Pezl as chief of staff, then replaced him with Jiri Nekvasil, a colonel promoted from the ranks. First Deputy Defense Minister Jiri Pospisil has developed a personnel management system for military careers, initiated further "screening" of military cadres (for political reliability and military competence), and the General Staff has no holdover from the communist period. The armed forces have been greatly reduced in size (from 106,400 in January 1993 to 65,000 by end of 1995) and been restructured to corps-brigades to accommodate integration into NATO.

During 1994 Parliament approved the training and exercising of Czech armed forces on foreign soil and foreign troops on Czech soil. At the end of the year, it approved the Army's Long-term Acquisition plan and a new "Military Strategy" document.

In sum, of the four Central European states, the Czech Republic seems to have made the most progress in developing effective "civilian" defense ministry control of the military. The president and Parliament have deemed the armed forces to be reliable, and the armed forces have publicly apologized for previous interference in Czech society. The Czech Republic, however, still faces two constitutional tasks: First, what to do with the Senate, the upper house of its Parliament; second, and more important, how to correct a significant constitutional ambiguity. The (German-model) president, as "supreme commander of the armed forces," must get the prime minister's approval for employing forces and to commission and promote generals. Since the president's emergency powers can cause confusion during a crisis, this needs to be rectified.

Slovakia. In contrast to the Czech Republic, political instability has characterized Slovakia, which is now on its third government in less than two years, and has hampered its more daunting military tasks and reform efforts. In many ways Slovakia's January 1993 independence has thrown the country back in time. Slovakia must build its institutions from scratch; a new defense ministry, an Army command (now General Staff), and armed forces.

During the first Vladimir Meciar-coalition government (January 1993-March 1994), military reform was hampered by government instability and crisis. Nevertheless, it created a National Security Council, and approved two key documents: Principles of National Security and a Defense Doctrine.

Military reform efforts were evident during the Jozef Moravcik-coalition government (March-December 1994), which named a civilian defense minister (Pavol Kanis) and revised Slovakia's Defense Doctrine (placing greater stress on NATO integration), changed the Army Command to a General Staff, restructured and reduced the size of the defense ministry and General Staff (to reduce tensions that had developed because the larger Army Command had been formed first), and restructured the armed forces into corps and brigades.

The key question, though, is whether these initial reform efforts will continue under the new Meciar-coalition government (that emerged from the October 1994 elections) during 1995. First indications (Meciar's campaign to unseat president Kovac) suggest renewed political instability and potential constitutional challenges.

Whether or not Slovakia is able to advance its initial defense reform efforts, it does need to fix its constitution, which stresses national rather than civil rights. This emphasis exacerbates ethnic tensions within Slovakia as well as with neighboring Hungary. The real question will be whether the Meciar-coalition government will be able to provide enough stability so that Slovakia can continue the defense reforms established by the Moravcik-coalition government. The first indications are discouraging, particularly if Meciar pursues his efforts to remove the president.

To conclude, if NATO does determine in December 1995 that "effective" democratic control of the military is a necessary condition for Alliance membership, then it appears that Central Europe has significant work to do. All four Visegrad states have made notable progress in establishing real Parliamentary oversight of the military and in restoring military prestige to their respective armed forces. The common problem of resource scarcity has uniformly limited the development of Central Europe's armed forces modernization and compatibility with NATO.

Poland and Hungary need new constitutions to address fundamental civil-military problems that still exist, notably presidential and governmental powers in peacetime and war must be clarified. The Czech Republic needs to amend its constitution to clarify the President's role for employing forces during emergency, and Slovakia needs to amend its constitution regarding civil rights. Only with this constitutional clarification, can *real* governmental (civilian defense ministry) control of the military occur in Poland. Hungary must face the question of how to assert effective "civilian" defense ministry control over its armed forces, and Slovakia must actually jump-start its defense reform.

Endnotes

1. This is a point made by Shlomo Avineri, "The Return To History: The Breakup of the Soviet Union," *The Brookings Review* (Spring 1992), pp. 30-33.

2. *London Declaration On a Transformed North Atlantic Alliance* (Brussels: NATO Information Service, July 5-6 , 1990), Articles 7 and 8.

3. See Stephen F. Szabo, "Federal Republic of Germany: The *Bundeswehr*," in Jeffrey Simon (ed.), *European Security Policy After the Revolutions of 1989* (Washington, DC: National Defense University Press, 1991), pp. 189-206.

4. Statement Issued By the North Atlantic Council Meeting in Ministerial Session, Copenhagen, June 6-7, 1991 in *NATO Communiques 1991* (Brussels: NATO Office of Information and Press, 1992), pp. 22-23.

5. North Atlantic Council Statement, August 21, 1991 in *NATO Communiques 1991*, pp. 24-25.

6. *Rome Declaration on Peace and Cooperation*, NATO Press Communique S-1(91)86, November 8, 1991, Article 11, pp. 4-5.

7. For a thorough overview, see Stephen J. Flanagan, "NATO and Central and Eastern Europe: From Liaison to Security Partnership," *The Washington Quarterly* (Spring 1992).

8. "Work Plan for Dialogue, Partnership and Cooperation," NATO Press Communique M-NACC-1 (92)21, March 10, 1992.

9. "Final Communique issued by the North Atlantic Council in Ministerial Session," NATO Press Communique M-NAC-1 (92) 51, June 4, 1992, p. 4.

10. "Statement Issued At the North Atlantic Cooperation Council in Oslo, Norway," NATO Press Communique M-NACC-1 (92)54, June 5, 1992, p. 2.

11. "Final Communique issued by the North Atlantic Council in Ministerial Session," NATO Press Communique M-NAC-2(92)106, December 17, 1992, p. 2.

12. "Statement issued by the Meeting of Defense Ministers," NATO Press Communique M-DMCP-1(93)28, March 29, 1993, p. 3.

13. "Final Communique issued by the North Atlantic Council in Ministerial Session," NATO Press Communique M-NAC-1(93)38, June 10, 1993, pp. 2-3.

14. "Report to Ministers by the NACC Ad Hoc Group on Cooperation in Peacekeeping," NATO Press Release M-NACC-1(93)40, June 11, 1993, pp. 8-11.

15. "Statement Issued by the North Atlantic Cooperation Council in Ministerial Session," NATO Press Communique M-NACC-1(93)39, June 11, 1993, p. 1.

16. "NACC High Level Seminar on Peacekeeping," NATO Press Release (93)45, June 25, 1993.

17. "Declaration of the Heads of State and Government issued by the North Atlantic Council in Brussels, Belgium," NATO Press Communique M-1(94)3, January 11, 1994, pp. 2-3. The declaration stressed the development of separable but not separate capabilities.

18. NATO's January 11, 1994 Declaration noted: "We expect and welcome NATO expansion that would reach democratic states to our East, as part of an evolutionary process, taking into account political and security developments in the whole of Europe." Ibid., p. 4.

19. Ibid., p. 5.

20. Warsaw PAP, January 7, 1994. *FBIS-EEU-94-006* (January 10, 1994), p. 1.

21. *RFE/RL Daily Report*, No. 6 (January 11, 1994), p. 3.

22. Defense minister Piotr Kolodziejczyk interview, Paris *Le Quotidien de Paris*, January 10, 1994, p. 14. *FBIS-EEU-94-007* (January 11, 1994), p. 25.

23. Lech Walesa interview, Prague *Lidove Noviny*, January 10, 1994, pp. 1,5. *FBIS-EEU-94-008* (January 12, 1994), p. 23.

24. Prague CTK, January 12, 1994. *FBIS-EEU-94-010* (January 14 , 1994), p. 1.

25. Warsaw *Rzeczpospolita*, January 19, 1994, p. 2. *FBIS-EEU-94-012* (January 19, 1994), p. 20. The Polish Army comprised roughly 225,000 soldiers; 87,000 professionals, 138,000 conscripts, and 89,000 civilians. Warsaw *Rzeczpospolita*, January 26, 1994, p. 2.

26. Antwerp *Gazet Van Antwerpen*, February 3, 1994, p. 5. *FBIS-EEU-94-024* (February 4, 1994), p. 17.

27. Warsaw Radio Warszawa Network, February 15, 1994. *FBIS-EEU-94-032* (February 16, 1994), p. 25.

28. Warsaw PAP, May 26, 1994. *FBIS-EEU-94-102* (May 26, 1994), p. 15.

29. Warsaw TV Polonia Network, July 5, 1994. *FBIS-EEU-94-128* (July 5, 1994), p. 22.

30. Warsaw *Gazeta Wyborcza*, July 6, 1994, p. 8. *FBIS-EEU-94-130* (July 7, 1994), pp. 17-19.

31. *RFE/RL Daily Report*, No. 128 (July 8, 1994), p. 3.

32. London *Financial Times*, May 16, 1994, p. 3.

33. *RFE/RL Daily Report*, No. 173 (September 12, 1994), p. 4.

34. Hamburg DPA, July 28, 1994. *FBIS-WEU-94-150* (August 4, 1994), p. 15.

35. Berlin DDP/AND, September 1, 1994. *FBIS-WEU-94-170* (September 1, 1994), p. 16.

36. They met in Warsaw in July, and for the fourth time in Bamberg in September.

37. General Henning von Ondarza interview. Warsaw *Gazeta Wyborcza*, August 9, 1994, p. 3. FBIS-EEU-94-153 (August 9, 1994), pp. 20-21.

38. Warsaw *Polska Zbrojna*, September 12, 1994, pp. 1-2. *FBIS-EEU-94-177* (September 13, 1994), p. 19.

39. Budapest MTI, January 13, 1994. *FBIS-EEU-94-010* (January 14, 1994), pp. 9-10.

40. On December 5 the Hungarian Parliament accepted the IPP by a vote of 236 for, and one abstention.

41. Budapest MTI, September 1, 1994. *FBIS-EEU-94-171* (September 2, 1994), p. 10.

42. Defense Minister Gyorgy Keleti interview, *Magyar Nemzet*, October 15, 1994, p. 7. *FBIS-EEU-94-201* (October 18, 1994), pp. 23-24.

43. Instead, Hungary sent two observers.

44. Gyorgy Keleti interview, Budapest Duna TV, November 20, 1994. *FBIS-EEU-94-225* (November 22, 1994), p. 18. Hungary committed 400 million forints ($3.5 million) for the PFP program for 1995. *OMRI Daily Digest*, January 4, 1995, pp. 4-5.

45. *FBIS-EEU-94-117* (June 17, 1994), p. 13.

46. Prague CTK, March 7, 1994. *FBIS-EEU-94-049* (March 14, 1994), p. 8.

47. Prague Radiozurnal Radio Network, May 29, 1994. *FBIS-EEU-94-104* (May 31, 1994), p. 18.

48. Prague CTK, August 3, 1994.

49. Prague CTK, October 12, 1994. *FBIS-EEU-94-199* (October 14, 1994), p. 5.

50. Wilem Holan, Prague *Lidove Noviny*, November 19, 1994, p. 5. *FBIS-EEU-94-226* (November 23, 1994), p. 2.

51. Pavol Kanis May 24, 1994 interview, Bratislava Rozhlasova Stanica. *FBIS-EEU-94-101* (May 25, 1994), p. 6; and Defense Doctrine of the Slovak Republic text, Bratislava *Slovenska Republika*, October 11, 1994, p. 10. *FBIS-EEU-94-200* (October 17, 1994), p. 8.

52. Prague CTK, June 1, 1994. *FBIS-EEU-94-106* (June 2, 1994), p. 14.

53. Final Communique, North Atlantic Council, December 1, 1994. Press Communique M-NAC-2(94)116, p. 3.

54. Chairman's Summary of North Atlantic Cooperation Council, December 2, 1994. Pres Communique M-NACC-2(94)117 (December 2, 1994), p. 1.

55. Budapest MTI, December 2, 1994. *FBIS-EEU-94-233* (December 5, 1994), p. 11.

56. "Final Communique Issued by the North Atlantic Council in Ministerial Session," NATO Press Communique M-NAC-1(95)48, May 30, 1995, p. 3.

Part II

Perspectives of European Union/Western European Union Associate Partners

---

4 A View From Poland
Andrzej Karkoszka

5 A View From Romania
Ioan Mircea Pascu

6 A View From Lithuania
Eitvydas Bajarunas

DR. ANDRZEJ KARKOSZKA

Dr. Karkoszka is the Director of Department of International Security, Ministry of Defense. Before assuming his present position, he was Advisor to the Minister of Defense. From 1990 to 1991, Dr. Karkoszka was Advisor in the Chancellory, Office of the President of Poland. Between 1984 and 1990, he was an expert on the UN Secretary General Group of Governmental Experts on Non-nuclear Zones, UNIDIR Expert Groups on Outer Space, and on Verification of Disarmament. Dr. Karkoszka was a member of the Polish Delegations to the UN GA annual session (1971), the MBFR Negotiations in Vienna (1973), the Conference on Disarmament, Geneva (1983-1985), and to the BW Convention Review Conference (1986). He earned an MS in Applied Enthomology, Agricultural Academy, Warsaw, Faculty of Journalism, Warsaw's University and a Ph.D. at the Polish Institute of International Affairs.

A View From Poland
4

Andrzej Karkoszka

A snap-shot of today's Europe reveals a continent accelerating its history and closing quickly on decisions, which, in all probability, are going to settle Europe's destiny for many decades ahead.

A number of processes culminating in contemporary Europe originated long ago, such as the political and economic integration of the Western European states. Others, like the transformation of NATO, reintegration of the post-Soviet area, and modernization of the states in the center of Europe, are fairly recent developments. Whether old or new, these processes are no longer guided by the traditional, post-war mechanisms of a bipolar world. Instead, the guiding principles seem to be a mixture of rejuvenated notions of national interests, balance of power, spheres of influence and interests of international organizations, rules of international law, and widely accepted (political) norms of international behavior.

While the first set of these guiding principles is more akin to the ancient environment of a multipolar world and may signal old troubles, these principles are visibly moderated, hopefully even over-powered, by the more recent principles of growing interdependence of nations, indivisibility of their security, and the interests of the international free market.

It remains to be seen which of these diverse factors will prevail in Europe's future. The outcome may have a vital importance for a number of small- and medium-sized European states which—like Poland—are not yet firmly anchored in existing multilateral institutions. These small- and medium-sized states may join multilateral structures and thus secure their existence and speed up their national development. However, some states may be left outside or may attain only token cooperative links with these structures, thus remaining retarded, isolated, and insecure. The negative consequences would increase significantly if and when such a separation coincided with the acceleration of the West European integration.

The Context of Poland's Security

Through Polish eyes, Europe continues to be divided. In place of the former "iron curtain," divisions exist between rich and poor, secure and insecure, and stable and volatile areas. The further to the east and south of the continent, the greater the uncertainty and instability.

The revolutions of 1989 heralded the end of a difficult period of foreign domination and raised hopes of economic and social progress. At the same time, for Poland and a number of other states in the region, the 1989 revolutions marked a return to life in a "gray area" between an affluent, secure, and selfish West and an unstable, unpredictable East. For the average Pole, the new situation brought back memories of the period before 1939 when Poland stood alone, between and against her two powerful neighbors Germany and the USSR. The desire to break out from this geopolitical predicament is the strongest motivation for Poland's willingness to experience the pains of economic reforms and for its pro-Western drive. This is also Poland's main argument for joining NATO.

The Polish desire to join NATO is not, however, some kind of a fixation with its military role nor the only means to reach close integration with the West. The Polish agenda begins with internal transformations and includes engagement with all other Western institutions. The military factor does not occupy a primary position in all these efforts.

There is no perceptible direct threat to Poland's security at present or in the immediate future. Taking into consideration the last three centuries, this is a unique situation for Poland. None of Poland's neighbors is pursuing a policy of aggression or animosity. Though some of their military potentials are much greater than Poland's, they are limited by the existing European arms control and confidence-building agreements.

Poland and her seven neighbors have signed state-to-state treaties on friendly relations, recognition of borders, protection of ethnic minorities, as well as several lower order agreements, including the so-called framework agreements on cooperation in defense matters. The scope of cooperation and the political content of relations are not, of course, identical with all the seven states. With some—Germany, the Czech Republic, and Slovakia—the interaction is very intensive and warm; with others, just normal. What matters is that there are no outstanding issues of contention which might be seen as a potential cause of bilateral conflict.

In contrast to this optimistic assessment of the present situation, the long-term analysis of Poland's external security looks more bleak. The whole land-mass beyond Poland's eastern border is in flux. A number of new successor states emerged from the Soviet empire, and their existence and vitality remain uncertain. All are undergoing difficult transformation processes and strong controversies continue to exist among them. Of course, the future of Russia is most unpredictable; she is a superpower still not reconciled with her new, circumscribed role.

While every East European state confronts a similar task of assuring long-lasting security for itself, Russia's dilemma—with its location, size, demographic, and economic potential—is quite different. Russia remains a global and nuclear power. None of the other Eastern European states can endanger Russia's vital interests; the most they can do is to contradict her "lower rank" interests. None of them—not even all of them acting together—can "isolate" Russia from the outside world. The biggest threat to Russia is Russia herself—that is, Russia's internal instability and the centrifugal forces inside the Federation. As a result, the security of every state in her vicinity is decisively shaped by Russia's external policy.

A democratic Russia, acting in accordance with international standards (that is, pursuing a friendly, mutually beneficial cooperation with her neighbors and other states), could have a powerful positive influence on Europe and Asia, becoming also a valuable political and economic partner for the Western states. Russia could become a pillar of the European and Northern hemisphere security system. There are indications that the present Russian leadership wants to create such a modern, powerful, yet benign state. There are, however, strong reasons to doubt whether Russia is unequivocally heading in this direction.

Since the parliamentary crisis in the Fall of 1993, Russia has been sliding back to her classic security doctrine that the well-being of the Russian state depends on territorial or political expansion, leading to domination of adjacent states. Such a doctrine presupposes the overt or covert use of political or military force and economic instruments of persuasion. The most conspicuous indicators for the future are these:

- Russia's perseverance in recreating close military networks within the Commonwealth of Independent States (CIS),
- her insistence on establishing military presence in the Caucasian

and other republics,

- Russian military involvement in virtually all internal conflicts taking place around the Federation's borders,
- her new and quite revealing defense doctrine,
- the growing political influence of the armed forces and of the military-industrial complex within the state,
- the atrocious conduct of war in Chechnya.

These symptoms of Russia's return to an assertive security policy are even more disturbing after the lessons brought about by the collapse the Soviet Union—Russia is over-extended, over-militarized, and economically retarded despite the dramatic improvements in the West's attitude, exemplified by its financial assistance and political good will. Even when Russia's behavior is explained by the trauma of lost "superpower-status" and sphere of influence, one cannot escape a feeling that this penchant for domination and special rights remains deeply ingrained. This penchant may prevail in Russia's future security policy if unopposed and not eradicated by rational efforts. For Poles to have such concerns is not an attitude of Russophobia. To prepare for such eventuality is only prudent, particularly by nations which have experienced the weight of centuries of Russian domination.

In sum, the long-term vision of Russia's potential hegemonic desires makes it mandatory to forestall them. Central Europe's integration with NATO seems the most efficient and abiding way to hedge against future pressures from Russia. Moreover, Poland is convinced that only as a full-fledged member of the Alliance will she be able to cultivate the relations with her powerful neighbor without fear of domination.

Poland's Four Security Options

After 1989 Poland, as all other East European and the post-Soviet states, faced a number of theoretical security policy options.

First option. Rebuild the old links with Russia, with a hope to restore the credibility of Russia's security guarantee. The essential condition for this option would be full political and legal equality in future relations between the two states. Due to Poland's historical experience, this condition has special importance. However, the validity of this option cannot be judged on the basis of history, on wishful thinking, or political declarations. Present Russian policy, however, can be the only basis for a rational assessment. In particular, what matters is Russia's internal development towards democracy and a strong economy, engagement in conflicts with neighbors, and attitude toward other nations aspiring toward independence. When judged by these criteria, this option does not look very plausible.

Second option. Pursue neutrality and self-defense. For Poland, located in the middle of the continent and between larger and more potent neighbors, the following theoretical conditions to make neutrality and self-defense credible, need to be fulfilled: first, a powerful economy; second, a well-functioning system of a pan-European collective security. Neither of these conditions exists at present and are not likely to in the foreseeable future.

Third option. Build a regional security system among the small- and medium-sized states surrounding Poland. This option presupposes a common will of the states concerned and cohesion in their foreign and security policy. Again, despite the existence of various regional economic and political initiatives (e.g., the so- called Visegrad Group, the Central European Initiative, or the Council of the Baltic States), the states taking part in these ventures have no desire to create a separate security alliance.

Fourth option. Pursue integration with the Euro-Atlantic security system, the only functioning and well-proven grouping of states, based on commonality of values and interests. The conditions here seem equally straightforward as they are demanding. Poland must be ready to fulfill all the internal political, legal, and economic standards required for membership and be accepted by all the members of the system. This option is the most advantageous as it not only provides for Poland a credible security guarantee, but also assures it accelerated economic and social development. Polish society has solemnly adopted this option, as evidenced by countless public opinion polls and the actions of all the consecutive governments of Poland since 1990.

Within the fourth option several parallel paths of action exist since the "Euro-Atlantic community" is composed of NATO, Western European Union (WEU), European Union (EU), and several other institutions. Poland strives to establish the closest possible links with each of these institutions, believing in a synergistic interaction between them.

For Poland there is no contradiction in applying for membership in NATO and the WEU at the same time. Eventual membership in both may solidify Poland's security guarantee and may permit more practical participation in their probable activities to promote stability and peace. Moreover, together with these efforts to join NATO and the WEU, Poland wishes to develop strong bilateral ties with all West European and North American states. As far as military and security cooperation is concerned, Poland has found a particularly friendly response from the United States, France, Germany, Great Britain, and the Netherlands. Poland is also determined to continue the existing trilateral schemes of military cooperation—one with France and Germany, and another with Germany and Denmark.

One Polish argument often raised for choosing the Euro-Atlantic option of security policy is the assertion that integration with NATO or other Western security organizations, due to their democratic internal procedures, does not entail a status of inferiority for Poland. Some argue quite to the contrary: that Poland's eventual membership in NATO, WEU, and European Union might be the best mechanism to avoid domination of Poland, this time by a powerful German economy. The prospect of Germany's preponderant influence need not be detrimental to Polish security. It would be, however, a psychological consolation to be able to count on multilateral institutions that place all participating states on an equal footing and provide a measure of protection in a potential dispute.

An important reason for choosing the Euro-Atlantic option is the need to provide political and moral support for Polish society, which is undergoing painful and demanding reforms. If membership in the European Union and other West European institutions is seen as furnishing a kind of *de facto* guarantee to the success of these transformations, it is only NATO membership which can give a truly credible assurance. Moreover, only NATO can help on a larger scale in the modernization of Polish armed forces. Although modernization will proceed regardless of whether or not Poland will become a NATO member, its pace and scope will differ substantially. The difference stems not so much from any expected influx of financial assistance, but more from the influence NATO exerts on this modernization, be it in the domain of democratic control over the armed forces, defense planning processes, sophistication of educational and training regimes, adaptation of modern technical norms and standards, or in arms procurement cooperation. Polish armed forces can be transformed more efficiently and with more purpose in consonance with NATO than if Poland pursued the process independently.

Poland and Partnership for Peace

Poland's aim to join NATO as soon as possible has been set by the supreme state authorities in 1992 in two documents: "Premises of Polish Foreign Policy" and "The Defense Strategy of the Republic of Poland." For Poland, NATO's January 1994 Partnership for Peace (PFP) initiative was a sobering event. PFP postponed the implementation of Polish aspirations and made it apparent how difficult it will be for Poland to attain the stated goal of membership.

NATO's decision to launch the PFP program was a complex compromise between several contradictory interests.

- Eastern Europe's strong desire for a rapid admission
- NATO states' resolve to do nothing that may strain the cohesion of the alliance and/or antagonize Russia
- the NATO states' willingness to engage the East Europeans, including Russians, in a cooperative venture
- the American wish to develop priority relations with Russia while boosting the reforms in Central and Eastern Europe and fortifying the U.S. leading role within the alliance
- Russia's interests to slow down the integration of Central and Eastern Europe with the West until she recuperated as a global power and to prevent her self-isolation from European processes.

Poland's understanding of the complexity of interests involved in NATO enlargement has led Poland to put aside its initial displeasure and, instead, decide to join PFP seeing it as the only possible way to NATO.

NATO's adoption of PFP as a potential route towards membership amounts to a choice between two integration options. The first option, implemented in the years 1949-1982 when NATO grew from 12 to 16 members, was based on a political decision, then followed by years of cooperation in building up of the military infrastructure. Now, in radically changed circumstances, eventual NATO membership is to be a final, though not inevitable, step taken after a prolonged political and military evolutionary process, connected with the broader process of integration with other Western organizations.

A NATO decision on admission will probably depend on a partner's activities with the Alliance and on its internal economic and social development. It is likely that formal membership, based on such an organic affinity, may become less objectionable to Russia. Through Polish eyes, this approach has one major weakness: it is going to be a prolonged process, contingent on available financial resources, and on sustained long-term political determination of society. Polish society's pro-Western attitude is for the long term, and it will be fortified as Poland's economy integrates with the Western market. This should permit Poland to maintain fairly large outlays for defense, despite the current budgetary stringency caused by feebleness of the national economy.

For Poland, the importance of the time-factor stems not from threat, but rather from knowledge about the urgent necessity to modernize the country's defense potential. Poland's decisions on modernization and force restructuring must be taken soon; the earlier that Poland knows whether it has to go it alone or can count on a division of labor and assistance, the more rational and quicker the results. The postponement of Poland's modernization decisions or their revision at a later stage may cause either irreversible losses in our defense potential (especially in the skilled personnel) or may add great costs.

Poland's Expectations of PFP

However, Polish perceptions of PFP's weakness fade away in light of three expected positive outcomes.

First, though Poland's participation in the PFP program does not assure admission into the alliance, it is seen as the only ticket towards the membership. Poland's participation in the program has been explicitly tied to this ultimate goal. In Poland's Presentation Document and Individual Partnership Program (IPP), Poland stated its desire to incorporate all operational forces with NATO military structures and to fulfill all obligations ensuing from such integration.

Poland's attitude amounts to a kind of over-interpretation of NATO's goals expressed in promoting the Partnership: expansion of cooperation, targeted on promotion of stability through peacekeeping. However, this difference in Poland's and NATO's approach has not raised any obstacle during the negotiations leading to the acceptance of Poland's IPP. It remains to be seen whether this divergence of intentions will cause disappointment in Poland, should the alliance refuse to expand and deepen cooperation. Poland's IPP for 1995, which has five times more events than the 1994 Program, seems to satisfy both parties.

Second, Poland supports PFP as an efficient mechanism for promoting regional stability. Since all of the surrounding states have acceded to the program and thus vowed to fulfill the basic requirements set forth in the PFP Framework Document (that is, democratic principles of government, affirmation of the UN Charter and the Helsinki Final Act, transparency of national defense planning and budgeting, as well as contributing to peacekeeping), the success of the program is in Poland's best interest. The Partnership has become a new instrument for stabilizing relations in Eastern Europe, as part of the slowly maturing security system of the continent.

Third, the PFP Program, while being all-inclusive, permits a self-differentiation of the East European national security policies. It permits self-delineation of the scope and depth of military cooperation with NATO and thus depends primarily on the state concerned. NATO was prudent in this arrangement, as it protects NATO from being accused of drawing "new lines" in Europe. Together with other European institutional efforts, the states of the region can independently and purposefully shape the degree to which they want to be tied to trans-Atlantic or West European institutions.

One of the most important aspects of self-differentiation is that it forces Russia to decide whether or not she wants to participate and, if and when she does, how closely or in what fashion to cooperate with NATO. Only Russia can isolate herself from the rest of Europe. If Russia's decision on cooperation is positive, so much the better; if it is negative, so much more clear will be the situation.

There is no need to dwell on the gravity of the repercussions of Russia's choice. Poland hopes for Russia's wide and intensive cooperation with NATO, both in the framework of Partnership and beyond. There could be no better proof of Russia's decision to proceed in her internal development and international relations. The Partnership requires tangible deeds, not empty declarations.

So far, despite Russia's formal accession to PFP, Russia refuses to implement a PFP individual program or any other cooperative agreement with NATO, making any such step contingent on prior knowledge about the future of NATO's enlargement. All prominent Russian politicians, generals, and diplomats state adamantly that NATO's future enlargement is incompatible with Russia's interests and thus contradictory to her vision of partnership.

The fact is that PFP and any form of NATO cooperation has scant support in Russia. This has been demonstrated in numerous areas: the weak Duma voting on accession to PFP; signals that such a cooperation could be a weapon in the hands of Russian nationalists; arguments that it could reduce Russia's freedom to resolve conflicts in the Commonwealth of Independent States at her will; suspicions raised by Russia's officer corps that NATO enlargement would jeopardize vital interests of their motherland.

It is to no avail to point out the incompatibility between Russia's position on NATO and her high expectations of economic assistance, financial support, large investments, and technology infusion from the West. It is to no avail that all Russia's friends try to explain to her representatives the fundamental mechanisms of NATO decision-making and the Alliance's defensive nature. There is no escaping the conclusion that Russia still bases her security policy on a centuries-long tradition of distrust of the West, cold-war premises of the balance of military power, and old stereotypes of NATO as a war-waging bloc. Russia still demands special rights to maintain a "sphere of influence" in East Europe. And, symptomatically, she undertakes no visible effort to avert or weaken these old paranoias.

The self-differentiating and open-ended character of the PFP program helps to ease any fears of creating new lines of political divisions in Europe after the infamous "iron curtain" has disappeared. A mosaic of different shades of security arrangements and perceptions will result from the freely woven web of formal and informal, state-to-state and institutional, cooperative links between East and West, of which PFP is the most prominent one. The ultimate mosaic will stem from formal security guarantees, *de facto* security assurances, economic and military agreements and, finally, from confidence and security building measures.

Such a security web will be of major significance when NATO ultimately decides to enlarge. In this regard, PFP's importance stems from the fact that inherently it seems to be the most dynamic and most promising element of a larger European process. The fortification and even expansion of PFP activities will be most needed just at the time when NATO enlargement may occur. For only then will those NATO aspirants who are not admitted into NATO, not feel abandoned or pushed away. They will believe that their chance to enter later will not be thwarted.

Regional Stability and NATO Enlargement Options

While it is premature to predict what enlargement scenario would have the best or worst impact on regional stability in Eastern Europe, it is worthwhile to clarify Poland's position on this issue. In general, enlargement must be decided independently by the 16 allies and the state concerned, without any influence from a third party. Only those states willing and politically ready should be considered for membership. The technical and military factors, though of importance, should carry less weight. Political readiness could be defined as having a fully democratic state and social system, mature rule of law and civil society, protection of individual and minority rights, democratic control over the armed forces, transparency of defense budgets and planning, good relations with neighboring states, respect for international commitments, and activism in international life to include participation in peacekeeping and conflict prevention efforts. This list of criteria is quite demanding; their full implementation in Eastern Europe is not yet accomplished. But only full respect for these requirements may assure the grounds for regional stability after a state's inclusion in NATO.

A second general Polish opinion about the impact of eventual NATO expansion on the region's stability is that the expansion must proceed in such a way as to preserve the credibility and cohesion of the Alliance itself. Thus no membership "a la carte" should be considered. Poland wants to be a full member of the alliance and of its integrated military structure, with full rights and obligations ensuing from such status. This commitment implies readiness to host, temporarily or permanently, foreign troops on her territory, depending only on the judicious decision of the allied states. Such a decision would not be provocative to the surrounding nations, as its modalities and justifications would be transparent and explained. It cannot, however, be predicted how the neighboring states would respond to such a move. Much depends on the neighbor's state of relations with NATO.

Finally, in considering the impact of NATO enlargement on regional security, it is useful to ask the opposite question; namely, what would be the impact of *not enlarging* NATO into the East European region over the coming decade? The net result of such a comparative analysis seems to favor unequivocally the early enlargement of NATO.

DR. IOAN MIRCEA PASCU

Dr. Pascu is the Secretary of State, Ministry of National Defense. He has been a Member of the Council of the Foundation "A Future for Romania" since 1992. He is also Head of the Security Studies Section of the Association's of International Law and International Relations, Bucharest, and a Member of the Council of the Euro-Atlantic Center, Bucharest. In 1993, he became a Member of the International Institute for Strategic Studies in London. Before his current assignment, Dr. Pascu was Professor of International Relations, Dean of the International Relations Faculty, The National School for Political and Administrative Studies. Between 1990 and 1992, he was Presidential Counselor, Head of the Foreign Policy Directorate, The Department for Political Analysis, The Presidence of Romania. From 1989 to 1990 he was a Member of the Foreign Policy Commission of the Council of the National Salvation Front. Dr. Pascu earned an M.A. from The Academy of Economics, Bucharest and a Ph.D. in Political Science from Institute for Political Sciences, Bucharest.

A View From Romania
5

Ioan Mircea Pascu

Transition has already taught us a number of important lessons. One of them is that man tends to yearn for things which he later regrets. In social terms, this signifies that progress is not always a straight line from point A to point B, but rather a trend over a long period of time largely subjected to unpredictability. For instance, during the Cold War Romanians complained about the significant threats derived from the superpower confrontation, while ignoring the value of stability. Today those threats are gone, but with them went stability too. If it is true that the well defined threats of the Cold War are gone (e.g., no European country fears a deliberate foreign aggression against it today), it is no less true that risks have not disappeared; to the contrary, they have even multiplied (e.g., the risk of foreign subversion).

However, these substantial changes were not evident initially. Rather, we countered these changes with our previous beliefs and convictions, which complicated the situation even further. Thus, the end of the Cold War was largely interpreted, particularly in the West, as a "victory." However, the "victors" soon discovered that the "vanquished" did not consider themselves as such. Moreover, the "vanquished" even claimed— and the "victors" accepted in fact—an equal place in the decision-making process shaping the post-Cold War world.

Such a situation was unthinkable in the aftermath of any war in which the victors fully imposed their will on the vanquished.[1] But the false assumption that the negative effects of the fall of communism could be contained exclusively in the eastern part of the continent because it had "lost" the Cold War, prevailed largely until the Moscow coup in August 1991. The dismemberment of the former Yugoslav federation later proved its lack of justification.

On a higher level, the best illustration of this incorrect thesis was the belief that change in general, especially negative change following the end of the Cold War, was entirely an affair of the East. At first, the West thought that it was simply immune to the "virus of change" only to find out that its consequences were not only external, but internal as well. Indeed, the persistent character of the economic recession, coupled with the need to adapt to a totally transformed world soon generated important internal changes even in the most developed states of the West.[2]

Some important political and military cycles in the West have reached their final point with their resources exhausted. Perhaps the changes in the East are more than what they first appeared to be; maybe they were not just the result of Western pressure, but rather the catalyst for change in the West itself. If such is the case, perhaps it is necessary—and even useful—to reconsider the nature of the entire post-Cold War East-West relationship.[3]

Myth and Security in Europe

Such a reconsideration is justified considering how quickly the euphoria produced by the fall of the Berlin Wall evaporated. In November 1989, we all strongly believed that all the obstacles preventing European integration has been removed—that new divisions would be unthinkable, the unity of the West would be preserved, the transition would be a 100-meter dash and not a marathon, and the importance of the former "East" was mainly economic, resulting from the new markets they offered to the developed countries of the West.

Now, five years after those euphoric moments, things look different. All obstacles have not been removed! New divisions are still possible (e.g., the NATO trend towards enlargement and the drive towards integration in the Commonwealth of Independent States), the transition is a marathon, the unity of the West is undermined by increased competition, and the importance of the former "Eastern" countries is part of the entire process of power re-distribution in world politics.

All these myths, including their fall, have not obscured the security problem of the continent. That problem is the general incapacity of the Central and Eastern European states' national resources to meet their security requirements. How can we project Western security and stability to the East and thus make up for the "security deficit" existing there? From the very beginning, there were only two answers: either build upon the Council on Security and Cooperation in Europe (CSCE) process (thus substituting for the loss of one of the East's previous "pillars," namely the Warsaw Pact) or enlarge the Western institutions—which had proved their vitality—towards the East.

We soon discovered that the first solution was unworkable. Because, even if modified, the CSCE is incapable of solely providing the continental security system that was needed under the new circumstances. As a result, the second solution was adopted and the Euro-Atlantic and European institutions have started to expand gradually towards the East. Consequently, the general security situation is better now than it was five years ago. The West continues to be fully protected by the Atlantic Treaty. Central Europe is "covered" by NATO's Article 4 by virtue of active participation in the Partnership for Peace (PFP) Program (together with the "Associate Partner" status offered to some of them by the WEU). States further East are covered by either a combination of PFP and CIS arrangements (e.g., Ukraine, Belarus, and Moldova) or only CIS. Of course, this general security assessment is relative, given the unpredictable course in the current conflicts in the former Yugoslavia and the former Soviet Union. There is also the enduring possibility that some of the current risks, including a potential break down of internal authority in Russia and/or Ukraine, might materialize. However, one could say that, in spite of all those risks, we are on the right track and enhancing "security."

The General Context of NATO Enlargement

In order to have a more accurate picture of NATO enlargement, we need to place it in the right context. First, NATO enlargement is part of the larger process of redefining the transatlantic relationship. Of course, there are conflicting views as to what that really means. Some in Western Europe say that the United States and Canada should continue to maintain a physical presence in Europe; others say that with the disappearance of the Soviet threat, this is no longer necessary. In the United States there are voices which maintain that NATO should be scrapped all together; others that NATO can only be saved by an infusion of "fresh new blood" (read new members). For Central Europe, both NATO and the U.S. physical presence on the continent are seen as indispensable. If there is a consensus among all our states, it is on these two points.

Second, NATO enlargement cannot be dissociated from Europe's effort to redefine itself and shape its new political, military, economic, technological, and commercial identity through the enlargement of its own institutions (particularly the European Union—EU—and the Western European Union—WEU) towards the East. This dimension is not lacking some problems either, especially with regard to the competition between Europe and the United States, and among the European powers themselves. However, it should be noted that, for obvious reasons, the common interest of all Central European states is that such competition—which had always existed in the economic field—should not be pushed and/or permitted to reach the political and military fields.

Third, the process of NATO enlargement is part of the more general process of creating a general, all-European security system. This process implies two elements. First, NATO enlargement, in spite of its strength, cannot become a substitute for the all-European security system; second, no other existing security institution would be able to meet that requirement alone. Rather, NATO enlargement should be pursued together with efforts to create an all-European system by bringing together all the existing organizations with responsibilities in the field of security according to an efficient "division of labor" between them.

Moreover, through the Partnership for Peace initiative (and its current missions in Yugoslavia), NATO has already performed two functions simultaneously: first, it continues to remain a military alliance for the 16 members (including those who will be accepted in the future); second, NATO acts as an embryo of a security organization[4] for the Partner countries actively engaged in pursuing the PFP Programs. Thus, while future enlargement appears to strengthen the military alliance function, it is also connected to the general effort to create an all-European security architecture.

NATO Enlargement: Possible Scenarios

In speculating about the future, it is useful to review the recent past in order to highlight some of the factors on which future enlargement might depend. In this respect, the fact that the August 1991 Moscow coup might have succeeded, has probably increased the West's awareness that the recently acquired independence of the former non-Soviet Warsaw Pact allies needs consolidation and safeguarding. As a consequence, the first public pronouncements suggesting the extension of NATO towards the East surfaced.

In the summer of 1993, President Yeltsin visited Poland and officially declared that Russia would *not*, in principle, be against Poland's future
admission to NATO. Later, Russian officials denied Yelstin's statements,
but the heat increased considerably, starting a real "race for NATO"
among the former non-Soviet Warsaw Pact allies. As a consequence, a
sort of "beauty competition," discretely encouraged by the would-be
"jury" (or at least by some of its "members"), was initiated. Some competitors—particularly the ones encouraged to think that they had the first
chance—were not so much preoccupied with their own performance, but
rather with efforts to ruin the chances of other competitors!

In the Fall of 1993, following a strong letter from President Yeltsin
and, perhaps, other appeals to reason, the formula of an early and selective admission was replaced by a wiser and more pragmatic Partnership
for Peace initiative, officially launched in January 1994. From that point
on, events have followed a more or less linear course, even if occasional
"flare ups" have erupted.

Although NATO enlargement has been officially presented as a
response to the manifest interest of the Central and Eastern European
states to be integrated into NATO, the truth is that the interest is mutual:
NATO *needs* these countries too! NATO needs new members either
because some NATO members see, for instance, Germany's justified
drive for "space" or because NATO wants new members feeling it needs
a transfusion of "fresh new blood" for "rejuvenation" (e.g., some
American opinion considers that NATO is practically dead and, therefore,
should be abandoned all together). Of course, the benefit of a "balanced"
view could be questioned, especially if one considers that, in its absence,
NATO could always claim to the Russians that it is not NATO who seeks
enlargement, but the Central European countries. If the Central
Europeans are the ones to push for membership, then NATO can hope to
diminish the Russian resistance.[5]

By adopting a "balanced" view, it would be easier and more pragmatic to see the real factors influencing the NATO enlargement process.
In general, there are three factors. First, there are the candidates' "credentials." Without credentials, one cannot even think of enlargement. The
criteria established by NATO for admission are obligatory. Moreover, one
should not even insist on discussing their substance, because they are not
negotiable (though their interpretation is!) and meeting them is only in the
interest of the candidate countries, helping them to more quickly achieve

their transition to democracy and market economy.

Second, there is the intra-Western balance of interests and power. One might venture to say that this is the most important issue with respect to NATO enlargement. Indeed, after firmly making the decision to enlarge—given both the impact of the Soviet threat's disappearance on allied unity and the consequent revival of individual national interests in the West—the concrete details of enlargement tend to get prominence.

Third is Russia's opposition to any enlargement.[6] In respect to Russia's opposition, one could note two issues: first, NATO's "dual-track" decision—to pursue enlargement parallel with establishing a strong and substantive security tie to Russia—is positive. This decision not only corrects the earlier noted moral imbalance, but also stands as an important step towards creating the new European security architecture, of which NATO enlargement will be a very important component. Russian opposition seems to increase as one gets closer to the former Soviet territory. This is significant when we assess the feasibility of the enlargement process.

Of course, the envisaged security tie between NATO and Russia is not indifferent to the candidates. It would be one thing to give the future committee a consultative role and a totally different one to give Russia a role in NATO's decisions and agree on how the future security architecture of the continent would look! This is so because Yalta and Potsdam are still very much in the memory of Central Europe, so anything which might even vaguely resemble these agreements would be totally unacceptable.

From NATO's perspective, enlargement poses certain requirements. First, if one wants to revitalize NATO, it is essential that enlargement should not dilute the organization. (Incidentally, this is also in the interest of the candidates, because they want to join a healthy organization).

Second, enlargement should avoid creating new divisions on the continent, which can occur either by selective group admission and/or by triggering a strengthened and potentially extended Commonwealth of Independent States (CIS). If division occurs, the chances for a unitary continental security architecture will be affected negatively; if not decisively compromised.

Third, in general, enlargement should try to eliminate existing obstacles rather than to create new ones. Meeting these rather restrictive requirements will not be easy. Indeed, these requirements require balancing a significant number of dynamic factors. Hence, these requirements provide a challenge for both members and candidates.

Meeting these requirements will be helped by NATO's future military build-up required to support the security guarantees to be extended to the new members. This, in turn, will depend on the future balance between NATO's military and political dimensions and NATO's relation to the general process of creating the new continental security architecture.

NATO's East and Southeast Enlargement Options

In regard to effective enlargement, we should remember that during the Cold War, NATO had only two direct borders with the former Soviet Union: in Norway and in Turkey. Neither is practical for further enlargement. Theoretically, that leaves NATO with only two other potential options: to move east and southeast from the present eastern German border and/or north from the Greek-Turkish border.

The advantages of enlargement eastward are as follows: First, it follows the West-East axis, which dominated the confrontation in Europe during the Cold War and, through inertia, continues to do so today. Second, it best serves Germany, which can add "space" between itself and the former Soviet territory. Third, it would comprise those countries who have moved away from Russia and are already seriously connected to the German economy. Theoretically, this would make eastward enlargement more acceptable to Russia.

The main disadvantage of NATO's enlargement to the east is that it would certainly create a new line of demarcation in Europe[7] and send the "wrong" signal to Moscow—that those states not included might be considered for Russia's own sphere of influence. Moreover, eastward expansion would create a military corridor beneath the "Visegrad" countries. The corridor would start in Russia, pass through Ukraine, Moldova, Romania, Bulgaria, and former Yugoslavia, reaching the southern border of Austria and/or the eastern border of Italy.

NATO's expansion northwards from the Greek-Turkish border, particularly if coupled with eastward expansion, has the main advantage that it would give additional geographical protection to NATO's troubled southern flank. Militarily, it would provide for a reserve in the important flank where troubles can easily arise. Naturally, there are disadvantages too, particularly the close proximity to Russia and the ongoing Yugoslav conflict.

The "Checkers" Enlargement Option

However, there might be another enlargement option which, though not free from difficulties, could combine advantages of the other two options. That option, which I call "the checkers approach," would consist first of the admission of only two Central European states; Poland and Romania. These two are the most important by territory, population, armed forces, and geostrategic location, and they provide Ukraine with two indispensable, reliable, and meaningful anchors for her independence.[8] The most important advantage, though, is that Poland and Romania's admission makes all the states between them and NATO's borders—the Czech Republic, Slovakia, Hungary, and Bulgaria—*de facto* members of NATO without having to make them *de jure* members too! Finally, as for their proximity to Russia, (which is considered a disadvantage), it should be noted that both "enjoy" a relatively similar situation in having to deal with Kaliningrad and the Black Sea. (Theoretically, Yugoslavia could replace Romania or Hungary.)

In reality, adopting any one (or combination) of these options depend mainly on what type of admission would ultimately prevail. At the moment, there exists "competition" between "group admission" and "individual admission." In view of Russia's likely strong negative reaction, if NATO chooses the "group" approach, it would be difficult to make the child take a second teaspoon of medicine, particularly if it was bitter! Therefore, if NATO chooses "group admission," it should be for all.

If "individual admission" prevails however, (which most "signals" seem to indicate), establishing priorities would be unavoidable. Under these circumstances, those countries not admitted first would need a strong guarantee that "admission" is a process that would not stop (either because of increased Russian opposition or by a veto from those already accepted) before they can also enter.

Romania and NATO Enlargement

Nicolae Ceausescu left Romania with a major handicap to overcome in "the race for integration" into Euro-Atlantic and European structures. At a time when all Romania's Warsaw Pact allies were desperately trying to move closer to the West, Romania marched in the opposite direction— towards Asia and the North Korean model! It was for this reason that one of the ten points of the Romanian Revolution stated clearly Romania's willingness to reintegrate with the European continent.

But sudden efforts could not instantly erase years and years of growing Western conviction that Romania was lagging far behind "the champions" of democracy and market economy. That is why, on all multilateral institution enlargement lists, the "Visegrad" countries have always been separated from Romania and Bulgaria, with the former Soviet space forming a third category.

However, Romania's willingness to sign the Partnership for Peace Initiative has apparently shattered that image of difference, perhaps even disturbed the Western institutions' initial planning in respect to enlargement towards the East.

Although there may be some truth in it, this opinion does not totally reflect reality because Romania's motivation was more profound. Romania did not want to impress the West. Romania took the Partnership for Peace for what it was publicly said to be. As indicated in NATO's January 1994 invitation, Romania first saw PFP as a necessary but not sufficient condition for admission into the Alliance. Second, Romania saw PFP as the perfect instrument for the required modernization of its armed forces—to include peace-keeping—through increasing its armed forces' contact with the developed NATO member countries. Third, Romania saw PFP as an important means to contribute to increased stability and security on the continent. Fourth, Romania saw PFP as an important means to improve relations with neighbors, given the significant and positive impact that military collaboration already had on the general bilateral relationship with Hungary.

If these were the PFP's motivations, one could say that Romania expects that PFP will continue along the same lines and will not question its utility. However, PFP should continue to remain the most important vehicle for integration into the Alliance, and to provide equal opportunity for admission to all participants who have expressed the wish to join.

As for Romania's reaction in case of admission or exclusion, Romania's response to admission would be positive—namely, Romania would honor her obligations fully. In that way Romania would be able to increase her contribution to peace and stability both in the area around her borders and in Europe,[9] given NATO's continued support of the process of reform.

As for Romania's exclusion from initial NATO membership, an

answer cannot be given. Perhaps one should speculate on the potential consequences. In addition to the already noted disadvantages of excluding Romania, there would be the need for a rather careful consideration of the internal consequences of exclusion.

After all Romania's courageous efforts to fully integrate with the West, if Romania is excluded it would probably become almost impossible to continue to motivate the Romanian public and electorate that this policy was the right one for the country. Certainly, one could argue that while we only speak of NATO, that there are other organizations too. Although Romania has already taken the necessary steps toward the EU and WEU, these will not be able to compensate—either in the short- or mid-term—for Romania's diminished security following exclusion.

But it would be premature to come up with final judgments for Romania. While it is true that very important decisions lie ahead, it is equally true that—given their importance—one need not rush. Rather, all of us—in the United States, Western Europe, Central Europe, Eastern Europe, and Russia—should cooperate and solve what is likely to be the most important challenge of our time, namely how to push forward with global integration and to build a new security architecture to serve us all now and for future generations.

Endnotes

1.   That was possible because the Cold War was not just another war, but rather a "special" kind of war, fought through competition rather than sheer physical combat, and because the degree of interdependence within the present international system was such that the exclusion of the "vanquished" from the process of shaping "the new world" was virtually impossible.

2.   See, for instance, the numerous government changes in Japan, the total collapse of the Italian political system, the pressures in France, and the dissatisfaction of the American electorate in the last mid-term elections.

3.   Some might say that using the East-West approach after the end of the Cold War is wrong. Actually, it is not because it has been the driving force of world politics for the most part of this century, and because its inertia continues to have an effect on world politics (e.g., Russia's present approach to NATO's enlargement).

4.   The difference between an alliance and a security organization lies in their functions. While an alliance is created by and directed at countering a rather well-defined external threat, a security organization addresses all the possible security risks.

5.   That leaves aside the question that Russian pressure concentrates mainly on the Central and Eastern European countries to deter them from joining NATO, which is, at least morally, unacceptable.

6.   Russia's motivations for resistance include the psychological difficulty of adapting to a lesser status; the negative economic effects from losing the Central European arms market; and finally, the increasing internal feeling that Russia has already conceded too much, which is drastically limiting most democratic Russian leaders' room for maneuver.

7.   It should be noted that if, even theoretically, there was a line dividing that part of the continent, then it might be between Central and Eastern Europe, with Eastern Europe circumscribed to the former Soviet space

(with the exception of the Baltic states—territories not belonging to the Slavic civilization, which were included later in the former Soviet Union). Politics, history, culture, former links to the West, experience with democracy and market economy differentiate these two areas.

8. It should be noted that the Ukraine's combined Slovak and Hungarian border is considerably smaller than Romania's which has the additional advantage that it lacks major minority problems, given the relatively small number of Ukrainians living in northern Romania and Romanians living in southern and south-eastern Ukraine.

9. That raises the problem of Russia. Romania has clearly stated that she does not treat admission to NATO as a "zero-sum game" with Russia because Romania's wish to join NATO does not stem so much from fear of Russia, as from desire to fully integrate with the West, which is the only source for meeting her long-term need to modernize. As a result, even after admission, together with all other member states, Romania will continue to maintain good and balanced relations with Russia, which should not be isolated, but fully integrated into the international system and world economy. Besides, by becoming a full member of those organizations, Romania will be able to melt her inevitably asymmetrical relations with the great powers of the West into the multilateral diplomacy of those institutions, as every other small- and medium-size member has for the past half century.

MR. EITVYDAS BAJARUNAS

Mr. Bajarunas is Deputy Head of Multilateral Relations Division of the Ministry of Foreign Affairs. In 1994, he was appointed by Decree of Government of the Republic of Lithuania as a member of the Working Group for PFP Coordination. He was appointed by Decree of the President of the Republic of Lithuania as a member of the Ad Hoc Working Group for preparation of "National Security Concept of the Republic of Lithuania" in 1993. Before his current assignment he was the Head of the Division of Information Service at the Ministry of National Defence and Head of International Organizations Division, Department of International Relations, Ministry of National Defence. From 1989 to 1991, he was Lecturer at Vilnius Technological University. From 1986 to 1991 he was assigned to the Institute of Physical-Technical problems of Energetics and Institute of Mathematics and Informatics (Lithuanian Academy of Sciences). Mr. Bajarunas attended the Vilnius University and was a postgraduate student at the Swedish Institute of International Affairs (Stockholm).

A View from Lithuania
6

Eitvydas Bajarunas

The end of the Cold War has created a new fluidity and openness in the whole pattern of international relations. This new fluidity is positive, since it means that many "Cold War" problems may now finally be resolved. But it also gives rise to many new dangers and risks which challenge the security of some (especially East) European states. In the coming decade, relations between the European Union (EU) and NATO (which will be enlarged towards Central Europe), and Russia and the Commonwealth of Independent States (CIS) will be the predominant dimension of European security. To a large extent, the security of the Baltic states will be dependent upon how this new post-Cold War East-West relationship develops.

Located in the geographical center of Europe, all three Baltic states—Estonia, Latvia, and Lithuania—have for centuries been the arena of confrontation between East and West, as well as North and East. But, at the same time, each Baltic state has remained an integral part of Europe's cultural, spiritual, and economic development, and cultivated traditions different from those of their eastern Slav neighbors.

Since the end of 18th century, when they were incorporated into the Russian empire, the Baltic states were subjected to political and, especially, cultural oppression combined with substantial Russification. Due to historical circumstances, all three Baltic nations regained independence in the aftermath of World War I. Their independence was again lost after the secret protocol of the Ribbentrop-Molotov Pact of 1939.

The Soviet Union forced the Baltic states to sign military agreements in 1939, then occupied these countries in 1940. After forced elections, the new Baltic parliaments requested inclusion of their states into the Soviet Union. Independence came to an end and sovietization began immediately: industries were nationalized and agriculture collectivized.

Worst of all, the Soviet authorities deported tens of thousands of citizens (mostly the intelligentsia) from the Baltics to Siberia and elsewhere. Between 1940 and 1953, the Baltic states lost about one third of their population. In 1944, the Soviet army occupied the Baltic states and an intensive guerrilla war started against the occupying Soviet authorities which, in some places in Lithuania, went on until 1953. Despite successive waves of Russian immigration, the Baltic states maintained their sense of national identity and separateness, finally re-establishing their independence and regaining international recognition in 1991, following the failed August coup in Moscow.

History has shown that the Baltic states lack the essentials to independently safeguard their national security and sovereignty. These countries are likely to be overrun in the case of a military attack. Therefore, the security of the Baltic states must be seen in terms of social coherence and survival in the long-term and must rest on something other than straight-forward military defense.

This fact also implies that the foreign and security policies of these states should go beyond setting up national armies. Several ideas for the Baltic states' foreign and security policy were expressed during the first years of independence. One of the first ideas was to develop close and institutionalized cooperation among the Baltic states. This has, among other things, resulted in the establishment of the Baltic Battalion (BALT-BAT) and the Baltic Council. Also promoted—for reasons of geography, culture, and history—was the idea of close relations with the Nordic countries. Ideas were elaborated of establishing a NATO-bis (defense organization of Central and Eastern European countries, such as Visegrad group, Ukraine, and the Baltic states) or even obtaining cross-guarantees from Russia and from the West. Finally, Ukraine promoted the idea of a Baltic-to-Black-Sea cooperation framework. All options to guarantee Lithuania's security—from the policy of neutrality, dependence on international organizations, or counting on security guarantees with certain countries—were unrealistic. This is why Lithuania made a clear choice—to seek membership in the European bodies, that is NATO, EU, and the WEU.

During the Baltic states' first years of independence, they tried to answer the question of what their place would be in the "new Europe." Although the Baltic states had been part of the former Soviet Union, most Baltic politicians now emphasize that the Baltic states belong to Central Europe. Nevertheless, the Baltic states share a number of characteristics which set them apart from other Central European states. First, the Baltic states face problems due to large Russian minorities within their countries, especially in Estonia and Latvia (in Latvia, Russians comprise 34 percent of the population; in Estonia, 30 percent; and in Lithuania only 9 percent). Moreover, the history of economic dependence means that the Baltic states cannot escape the Russian embrace as easily as Central Europe. Of course, the tradition of statehood makes them different from the other former Soviet republics; and most Russians acknowledge that the Baltic states are different and more "European" than the other states of the former Soviet Union.

In their search for a new identity, the Baltic states discovered that, despite many shared problems and concerns, they are very different. It is clear that the geo-political position of the Baltic states has in large part determined their common fate. Bordering the Baltic sea has brought the Baltic states great benefits and prosperity, but being a "bridge" between Russia and the West has brought many disadvantages and dangers. Of course, the main drawback has been that this territory has been the object of rivalries between powerful states; mostly Germany and Russia.

Despite the Baltic states' precarious geo-political location, their most important security problems arise from the consequences of economic and political transition (e.g., inflation and the fall in industrial production), as well as corruption in the state apparatus and various institutions, aggravated by divisions within recently formed governments and by the lack of political maturity.

Indeed, while the Baltic states have adopted new constitutions and held free elections, the day-to-day practice of democracy is still not up to western standards. Political parties are weak because after years of one-party rule, most people distrust the very idea of party membership. The societies and the political systems are under harsh economic pressure. Decisions needed to implement reform are very painful, so political leaders are hesitant to make them. Varying degrees of corruption distort the political process and erodes public faith in the power of democratic political decisions.

Our governments have demonstrated the ability to deal with many of these problems, but their ability to do so may depend to a large extent on factors outside their control. Organized crime is one of the most serious social problems and security threats the Baltic states face today. The continued inability of governments to tackle basic economic problems, coupled with the increase in organized and violent crime, may lead ordinary citizens to lose faith in democracy and market economy, especially if major Western countries and institutions remain cautious towards the Baltic states' aspirations to "join Europe."

The main external threats and risks to Lithuania's security today are connected with Russian and Commonwealth of Independent States (CIS) instability, which is characterized by inter-regional, ethnic-religious, territorial and/or social conflicts into which Lithuania can be drawn. Lithuania also faces the risk of Russia's meddling in Lithuania's internal affairs and return to expansionism.

According to a September 1994 public opinion survey,[1] Lithuanians are less concerned than they were in 1992 (prior to the Russian army's withdrawal from Lithuanian territory) that another country might attack them in the next few years. A 54 percent majority (compared with 46 percent in 1992) is not concerned about being attacked. But concern has increased since mid-1993 (from 25 percent to 39 percent), possibly because of increased Russian nationalistic rhetoric and recent Russian actions in Chechnya. Although the Baltic states do not face the risk of direct Russian threat to their territorial integrity (Lithuanians are divided over whether Russia poses a threat to their country: 46 percent say yes and 43 percent say no), Russia might very well attempt to use economic blackmail and pressure. Lithuania's economic dependence on Russia (especially on energy and other primary resources) is significant.

Russia remains one of Lithuania's biggest trade partners. In 1994 Lithuanian export to Russia was 26.2 percent of its total export; import from Russia was 43.9 percent of Lithuania's total. Due to double taxation policy, Lithuania's export to Russia significantly decreased since 1993 and Lithuanian companies had to find trade partners in the West.

Lithuania also faces the threat of nuclear accidents, terrorist activities, and uncontrolled refugee traffic and illegal migration, which is often accompanied by the smuggling of drugs, guns, radioactive materials, and other illegal goods. Since Lithuania's borders are relatively open and unprotected, an increasing flow of goods from Russia and other CIS countries is threatening to overwhelm the border and customs control.

Lithuania and NATO

Lithuania's security policy has pursued two main objectives. First, Lithuania should demonstrate its international presence by developing a wide network of international (and regional) relations, and by becoming an active member of all the relevant economic, political, and security organizations. By deepening bilateral and multilateral cooperation on security and defense issues, Lithuania intends to make it clear that it is not neutral, and that its priority is to become a full member of NATO, the European Union (EU), and Western European Union (WEU). Second, Lithuania seeks to develop good-neighbor relations with adjacent Baltic countries, Nordic states, Poland, Belarus, Ukraine, and Russia.

Lithuania, as do most other Central European states, views NATO as the main security guarantor in Europe. Lithuania, fearing instability in the East, is aware of the lack of an effective security architecture for the region. Therefore it is not surprising that in this atmosphere of drift, Lithuania clings to the most visible symbol of support, considering NATO to be the crucial safeguard against the unknown. It is important to understand that in applying for NATO membership, Lithuania seeks not only to obtain security guarantees, but also wishes to contribute to the common European efforts to ensure peace and stability, and to be an active participant in the EU, WEU, Organization of Security and Cooperation in Europe (OSCE), and North Atlantic Cooperation Council (NACC).

President Algirdas Brazauskas' January 4, 1994 official application for Lithuania's membership in NATO, provides Lithuania's leadership with a legal and political basis for pursuing membership. The letter emphasized that Lithuania was striving to "contribute to the security of the North Atlantic area."[2] The Seimas (Parliament), political parties, and general public supported the President. The above noted September 1994 public opinion survey indicates that 60 percent of the population approves of strengthening ties with NATO (only 13 percent disapprove). Nearly 52 percent supports Lithuania's membership in the PFP and 57 percent favors becoming a full member of NATO should the opportunity rise. Generally, Lithuanian society is very pro-EU and pro-NATO.

Lithuania perceives NATO membership as a very serious affair whereby the following requirements must be met: consensus of all the sixteen NATO member-states to provide Lithuania with security guarantees; and Lithuania's need to contribute with NATO to enhance security and stability in Europe. At the same time, Lithuania sees NATO enlargement as extending the zone of security and stability Eastward. With the outbreak of centers of instability on CIS territory (Russia), this process becomes increasingly important. Chechyna is one of the most recent examples of such instability.

Close ties with NATO are important for Lithuania not just for strictly military-related reasons, but NATO's involvement has a very positive impact on the economic security of Central European states. Close relations with NATO are seen as an element of stability and are expected to make the region more attractive to Western investors.

NATO's creation of NACC was the first signal that NATO was adapting to the post-Cold War security environment. The large majority of Central European states feel that NACC offers a number of opportunities to ensure better transparency and practical cooperation among former adversaries. Moreover, it has become an important forum for exchanging information on many types of security issues. NACC has boosted mutual confidence and helped fill a perceived security vacuum for Cooperation Partners.

For Lithuania and the other Baltic states, NACC is particularly important since it provides NATO assistance in forming the Baltic military structures, and ensuring the application of the Western model of democratic control over the Baltic defense forces. During the process of cooperation and consultations, the main emphasis is put on security; including peacekeeping, defense planning, democratic civil-military relations, and civil-military interaction in air traffic control and management. Lithuania supports the NACC policy of ensuring transparency among the European states. But at the same time, NACC has many limitations. NACC does not take into account the real diversity of the area of former Warsaw Treaty Organization in respect of stability, problems, and concerns.

The major question Central Europe continues to ask NATO is whether and to what extent NATO is prepared to face new challenges, perform new functions, and project its influence beyond its own present treaty area.

NATO enlargement is the issue that occupies the minds and emotions of many Europeans and North Americans. NATO's enlargement and transformation could be considered one of the most important tasks of this decade on whose success depends not only security and further democratic development of the continent, but also the realization of Central European hopes to live in peace. No doubt these peoples have the right to cherish their hopes because they had been hostages of the Cold War, and it was their determination that crumbled the wall that divided Europe for fifty years. Their resolution to implement the principles of democracy and free market are a promise of a brighter future for the whole Europe. This Central European thinking is sustained not only by the wish to be the masters of their own house, but also to contribute to the common architecture of Europe.

Lithuanians understand that joining NATO depends on the capability of a country to contribute to the overall security of the Alliance. An example that even a small country can contribute to overall European peace and security was provided in August 1994 when a Lithuanian platoon went as part of the Danish peacekeeping battalion to the UNPROFOR mission in Croatia. On December 2, 1994, the Meeting of Ministers of Foreign Affairs of the NACC approved a report of the Chairman of the NACC Working Group for cooperation in peacekeeping. This report named Lithuania as the first Central European state which started to carry out peacekeeping operations in an integrated structure together with NATO troops.

We understand that future members need to have democratic control over armed forces, a healthy and free market economy, no frontier or minority problems, good relations with neighbors, and to the commitment to operate with NATO forces. In this respect, I note the importance of the European Stability Pact recently signed in Paris. Inclusion of the main Lithuanian treaties on friendly relations and good-neighborly cooperation with neighborly countries—Russia, Poland, Belarus—in the Stability Pact very clearly confirmed Lithuania's image as a stable country.

How to Handle Russia's Problem

There now exists a long list of reasons why Central European countries, and perhaps particularly the Baltic states, should not join NATO in the next few years. First, it is argued that NATO's expansion could "isolate" Russia. Although this is an important argument, it is also rooted in "Cold War" thinking. Is it really possible to imagine that a superpower such as Russia can be "isolated"? It is not the West or NATO but only Russia that could isolate itself.

The second argument is that all military alliances are basically directed against an adversary. This implies that any strengthening of NATO is to be seen as negatively affecting Russia's security interests. From such a perspective, NATO's enlargement would create a *cordon sanitaire*, separating Russia from Central and Western Europe. Again, this reflects an outmoded way of thinking. The West should make it clear that NATO's enlargement will be primarily an eastward extension of stability, which can only be in Russia's interest.

Finally, the argument that Russian public opinion is not prepared for such a move and that NATO enlargement would seriously strengthen the radical and neo-imperialist tendencies in Russia is also not very convincing since Russia is too preoccupied with its domestic agenda and with reshaping its relations with other CIS countries. With the breakdown of the bipolar world, foreign policy questions (including NATO) have lost their significance. Average Russians are more inward orientated today; they are much more concerned with earning their living, the problems of social deterioration, and internal political developments.

Lithuania fully supports the position that Russia does *not* have a veto right with regard to NATO enlargement. At the same time, Lithuania is aware of democratic Russia's concerns regarding NATO's admission of Lithuania and other Central European countries. In Russia the image of NATO as being directed against Russia is still very widespread. This perception affects the attitude of Russian politicians towards NATO enlargement.

In December 1994, Russian Foreign Minister Andrey Kozyrev refused to sign an Individual Partnership Program (IPP) and another document guaranteeing enhanced dialogue on security issues. Recent U.S. administration proposals to form a special working relationship with Russia and even to form a standing consultative commission (some type of NATO-Russian Council) to keep Moscow informed of NATO's moves fully goes in the direction of "softening" the issue of NATO enlargement. However, Russia's arguments cannot prevail over the Central European states' interests. Lithuanian politicians are also trying to contribute to this clarification, so that Russia does not view Central Europe's integration into NATO as a threat. Russian politicians and the general public will both ultimately appreciate that NATO enlargement, that reinforces Central Europe's commitments to superiority of freedom, democracy, and law, will enhance stability and security in the region bordering Russia; the Baltic states and the Visegrad countries. By joining Western structures and simultaneously building good relations with the East, Central European countries help to bring the West closer to Russia.

Management of relations with Russia is the most serious and acute foreign and security policy challenge facing all three Baltic states. The worsening of these relations could be one of biggest drawbacks for membership in NATO. Baltic security will always be in jeopardy if a hostile and authoritarian Russia prevails. Our most serious problem is Russia's reluctance (or even unwillingness) to accept Baltic independence. Many Russians have been unable to come to terms with Baltic independence. In an August 1994 poll of 615 Russian military officers,[3] the officers listed Russia's enemies in the following order—Latvia, Afghanistan, Lithuania, Estonia, and the United States.

From the time of Peter the Great, Russians have believed that their natural western borders are on the Baltic sea, providing warm-water ports, a strategic position for the defense of northern Russia, and a "window to Europe." Baltic leaders are convinced that Moscow is desperately trying to keep the Baltic states firmly in its sphere of interest. It is equally believed that if the West does not respond to Russia's pressures vis-a-vis the Baltic states, or responds ambiguously, Moscow will be emboldened and will increase its pressure.

As former Swedish Prime Minister Carl Bildt noted: "Russia's policies toward the Baltic countries will be the litmus test of its new direction . . . Russian conduct toward these states will show the true nature of Russia's commitment to international norms and principles."[4] Russia's behavior towards the Baltic states is exemplified by its attempts to discredit Estonia and Latvia with claims that the "human" rights of ethnic Russians had been grossly violated there. Despite Russian pressures to prove opposite, investigations by OSCE's High Commissioner on Minorities and Council of Europe indicate there are no gross violation of human rights in the Baltic states.

Russia is one of the key actors in the Baltic Sea region; it is a considerable achievement that there are no problems between Russia and Lithuania concerning ethnic minorities, borders, or other complicated issues. The point of departure for building up relations between Russia and Lithuania is that no insurmountable problems exist.

The withdrawal of Russian troops from the Baltic states has significantly alleviated tensions in the region. However, Russian military forces are still present: military "retirees" and their families continue to reside in Latvia and Estonia;[5] Russian troops will continue to control the Skrunda radar station in Latvia for another four years, and a very significant Russian military presence exists in the Kaliningrad region. These factors make it difficult politically and strategically to bring the Baltic states to Western defense institutions.

The issue of the transit of Russian troops based in Kaliningrad through Lithuania continues to cause worries and suspicions. This is a relatively "new" issue since Lithuania had, until 1993, played down the military transit question, giving priority to the quick withdrawal of Russian troops from its territory (one year before the Russian army was withdrawn from Estonia, Latvia, and East Germany). With the Russian troops gone, Vilnius started working to restrict the quantity and types of Russian cargo and personnel to be transported through Lithuania and to prepare strict rules to manage transit in more a "more orderly" fashion. During 1993-94, the military transit across the territory of Lithuania was regulated by the provisions of the Lithuanian-Russian Treaty on the withdrawal of Russian troops from Germany, which expired in December 1994. During these two years, Russia engaged in a number of violations and irregularities, and at times, used Lithuanian air space without permission.

These problems made the need for a new legal basis for transit essential. So it was decided that from January 1, 1995, transit of military and dangerous goods could be governed by Lithuanian Government regulations adopted on October 3, 1994. On January 18, 1995 Lithuania informed Russia that the order which had been established by the Lithuanian-Russian Treaty on the withdrawal of the Russian troops from Germany would remain in force until December 31, 1995, with the possibility of extension for another one-year period. On January 18, 1995 the Russians accepted the Lithuanian proposal and the agreement on economic and trade relations (which includes most-favored-nation status).

Lithuanian authorities regard the transit settlement as a relative success. First, by solving the transit problem, Lithuania demonstrated its adherence and contribution to European security and stability. Lithuania will permit transit only on the basis of mutual understanding and goodwill among friendly states. Second, by solving the transit problem without signing a formal agreement (only the order of the military transit, established by the above mentioned Treaty on the withdrawal of the Russian troops from the Germany, continues to be valid), Lithuania demonstrated that it can protect its own interest. Third, we consider the non-provocative resolution of a very sensitive security problem as the only possible way to conduct relations with Russia. Obviously, the Kaliningrad question is only one of the issues in Lithuanian-Russian relations, but it illustrates how the future course of Russia (and the other CIS countries) will determine the nature of European security.

We believe that the criteria for NATO membership should be linked not to the reaction of neighboring countries, however important they may

be, but to the candidate-states' potential, political will, and ability to contribute to common security. Membership of Central and East European
states is not a "one-way street." It is important to make clear to Russia and
other CIS states that enlarging NATO is not directed against them, but a
widening of the West European zone of stability and prosperity which, in
the long term, is likely to have a positive impact on the CIS.

One way to avoid the misunderstanding that NATO's enlargement
might be perceived as excluding or even isolating Russia is to ensure that
enlargement is combined with a convincing effort to establish a special
security partnership with Russia. But it should be very clear that all
NATO efforts to conclude an agreement with Russia cannot change
Russia's attitude towards the West as long as no real integration of Russia
into the European structures takes place. It is necessary to find real means
to integrate Russia into Europe as well as to appeal to the responsibility
of Central European states to act as a "bridge" between East and West.
Without bridging the gap between the once advanced societies in Central
Europe and Russia, Europe would face new divisions which will lead to
stronger Russian resistance to enlargement of any European institutions.
If Russia's isolation is avoided, Russia's objections against enlargement
would probably diminish.

NATO-Russian strategic partnership is only one aspect of the whole
process; other European institutions, especially OSCE, should be
strengthened. Moreover, NATO-Russian partnership could be complemented by EU-Russian economic partnership. At the same time, NATO-
Russian relations should not "overshadow" NATO's relations with other
countries (e.g., Ukraine and Belarus). One example of Russia's psychological adaptation to the enlargement of European organizations can be
found in the strengthening of relations between the EU and Central
Europe; six of these countries have signed Europe agreements with the
Union. Although Russia is unlikely to be included in this circle, this does
not necessarily mean that Moscow should feel isolated. So long as the
EU's selection criteria are not made permanent, nothing should preclude
a close alliance with Russia in the future, and genuine cooperation now.

Inclusion vs Exclusion

While developing ties with European institutions, Lithuania, like the
other Baltic states, seeks to avoid isolation from the other Central

European countries, especially the Visegrad group. Both groups are making efforts to integrate into European political, economic, and security structures. Lithuania, like the Central European states, has the status of an associate partner in the WEU, which creates a precedent for equal treatment of all the Central European countries in their relations with the European bodies. Moreover, when all three Baltic states signed their association agreements with the EU in May 1995, they began to enjoy the same status as the other six Central European states.

Lithuania supports the idea that democratic Central European countries be given equal political opportunities to join NATO. In this respect, Baltic peoples feel uneasy when they hear about the alleged "indefensibility" of the Baltic states. This argument has no sound basis whatsoever. Lithuania is against any political differentiation based on this or any other argument. Lithuania would view it as a very negative development if NATO expresses reservations for any Central European country's membership. This would be understood as attaching the excluded states to another category and would influence their moves toward the EU and the WEU. It would also be a signal to Russia to expand its zone of influence into the region.

At the same time, we understand that NATO enlargement should be differentiated and assessed on a case-by-case basis. One of the biggest problems is that inclusion of some countries would mean the exclusion of others. NATO members should avoid creating an atmosphere of rivalry among eligible countries. When NATO decides to admit certain Central European countries into NATO, Lithuania would expect an explicit or implicit political commitment concerning its membership, or even a clear timetable and procedure for admission. At the same time, this would provide recognition that Lithuania, together with other Baltic and Central European states, has made significant progress toward establishing democratic institutions, free market economy, civilian control of the armed forces, and the rule of law.

NATO enlargement albeit to a few countries would be a very significant step. It would mean that NATO is serious about going eastwards. While Lithuania's security would increase by gaining proximity with NATO, Russia's pressure on countries initially excluded would increase.

If NATO decides that some Central European states are not yet ready to become full-fledged members, it may envisage a gradual enlargement.

In this case, it would be essential to avoid generating uncertainty among those countries. NATO must acknowledge their need for both political and psychological reassurance; something they cannot create by themselves. Countries with no immediate prospect of membership need a different form of commitment, such as associate member status. If NATO does not create such arrangements, enlargement will reduce and not improve security in Europe as a whole!

The purpose of associate status is to ease these countries transition to NATO membership. Associate status would also involve, among other things, greatly extended political consultations and a more rapid transfer of expertise. Central European states welcomed the EU Council's 1993 Copenhagen Summit declaration, which recognized that membership of EU associated states is also the objective of EU. The Essen Summit of December 1994 confirmed the EU's Pre-Accession Strategy. Lithuania expects NATO leaders to make a similar decision. Such a declaration would be especially valuable for those countries which will be excluded from the first round of NATO enlargement. It could be further developed into a NATO Pre-Accession Strategy that defines and specifies potential candidate-states.

NATO enlargement could proceed in three stages. First, the Central European states could participate in political consultation as envisaged in Article 4 of the Washington Treaty. Second, with NATO's armed forces, they could participate in UN and/or OSCE peacekeeping and peace-enforcement exercises and operations within the framework of Combined Joint Task Force (CJTF), take part in joint defense planning and standardize their defense systems. Finally, they could acquire security guarantees as envisaged in Article 5 of the Washington Treaty.

It would be desirable for countries involved in the first round of NATO enlargement to assume additional responsibilities—to act as a "security belt" for countries excluded from the first round, but eligible for future membership. New NATO members should cooperate with these countries. NATO should also prevent new members from blocking the membership of new states in the future. Finally, NATO should offer those states not yet ready to become NATO members more comprehensive and enhanced PFP cooperation, expanded bilateral relations, inviting them to participate in NATO operations on an *ad hoc* basis or within the framework of CJTF.

Why Partnership for Peace

It seems that the fundamental transformation resulting from NATO's January 1994 Brussels Summit was the attempt to deal with all eventual threats facing Europe: the possibility of a resurgent Russia, the outbreak of ethnic conflicts, and the increase in economic and political instability in Central Europe. Moreover, Partnership for Peace (PFP) was inclusive—all OSCE members were invited to apply. At the same time, it was made clear that PFP would be tailored to meet the needs and interests of each applicant.

Despite initial criticism (e.g., some argued that PFP is merely intended to "keep the Russians happy and the East Europeans hoping"), PFP has become an effective and powerful tool. First, the Partnership does not alter NATO's core mission of defense, nor does it interfere with NATO's integrated command structure. Moreover, PFP will help adapt and restructure NATO's capabilities and resources in such core areas as crisis management, humanitarian assistance, and peacekeeping. PFP also allows the partner states' forces to develop working relations with NATO forces as they plan, train, and exercise together. Hence, PFP allows Central European partners to demonstrate their willingness and eligibility for membership and implies that participation will make it easier to qualify for membership.

Although certain Partnership provisions, such as peacekeeping joint training and exercises, reflect developments already being discussed in the North Atlantic Cooperation Council (NACC). PFP goes further particularly in interoperability, which we at first misunderstood. Interoperability should be attained at the most basic level, through language training and common understanding. PFP also confirmed NATO's commitment to eventually enlarge, without, however, giving any specific timetable.

Lithuania was among the first countries to positively respond to NATO's PFP proposal—President Algirdas Brazauskas signed the Partnership for Peace framework document on January 27, 1994. Speaking at the 49th Session of the UN General Assembly on September 30, 1994, President Brazauskas noted that Lithuania had presented its formal request for NATO membership and that "expansion of NATO would not pose a danger to or threaten any European state."

Lithuania is aware that membership in NATO is not in the near future

and therefore seeks to develop practical ties with NATO; to work actively in NACC and within PFP. NACC and PFP constitute the basic instruments of practical cooperation between NATO and its former adversaries.
Lithuania understands that PFP's implementation is an intermediate step
towards Lithuania's full membership in the Alliance. PFP will help us to
gain time psychologically.

From the outset, Lithuania has welcomed the PFP initiative as a practical supplement to the NACC process, tailoring cooperative activities to
the needs and aspirations of individual partners. This individual approach
is especially valuable for Lithuania, which has to develop its military
establishment from scratch. The Partnership gives us a chance to adapt
our forces to NATO tasks, structures, and standards and to prepare our-
selves for future membership in NATO by undertaking cooperative activities in military planning, training, and joint exercises. This will help
Lithuania's armed forces reach a high level of compatibility so we can
eventually join NATO troops in conducting peacekeeping, humanitarian,
and rescue missions.

In the initial stage of Lithuania's independence, a large group of
politicians argued that Lithuania did not need national defense forces, that
establishing border defense and national guard-type forces, combined
with a strong police force would be sufficient. They assumed that
Lithuania should seek other sources of security and could not build its
forces from scratch because when Russian troops left Lithuania they took
all the available military hardware and destroyed everything else. This
position later changed to the belief that the country should establish its
own defense capabilities. The logical next question was how to defend the
country, and what should be the guiding principles?

Despite the fact that Lithuania's National Security Concept and
Defense Doctrine have not yet been adopted, armed forces are now being
created. Lithuania's defense system will be built around a few basic military concepts. One key principle is self-defense and is reflected in the
decision to introduce compulsory military service. Citizen self-defense is
seen as an essential means to reinforce the country's overall military
capability. Given Lithuania's geo-political position, great importance is
given to border controls and territorial defense. Lithuania's total armed
forces consist of approximately 7,000 men (an army of 6,500, navy of
400, and air force of 550). In addition, the National Defense Voluntary
Service ("Home Guard"-type forces) consists of about 12,000 volunteers

(plus 1,500 servicemen); and the Civil Defense department consists of 600 men.

The pillar of the army, the "Iron Wolf" motorized infantry brigade, consists of several battalions spread across the country and equipped with light weapons and several armored combat vehicles. The navy has "Grisha-III"-type light anti-submarine frigates, and the air force has more than 30 transport and several Czech-made attack aircraft (mostly designed for training). In times of peace, the armed forces monitor and protect state borders, territory, air space, and vital strategic objects; they can also assist civilian authorities in the event of natural calamities, rescue missions, and can participate in international military cooperation and peacekeeping missions. Lithuania's armed forces are seeking to develop the capacity to work closely together with West European countries in security and defense systems.

One of the main questions confronting Lithuania is how to restructure its armed forces to make them compatible with Western-type forces. This is not an easy task, especially since Lithuania is building its defense forces from scratch. Many Lithuanian officers, having served for decades in the Soviet Army, tend to think and act according to old-fashioned Soviet military doctrine and are unwilling and/or incapable of learning Western-style methods. Lithuania sees participating in international peacekeeping operations as an opportunity to get acquainted with Western organizational, legal, administrative, and equipment standards. Hence, Lithuania is interested in all peacekeeping mechanisms: UN, OSCE, as well as NATO and WEU.

Peacekeeping is also important as a regional Baltic activity. The establishment of a joint Baltic Peacekeeping Battalion (BALTBAT) has been a subject of discussions for a long time. The growing involvement of the Nordic States in the formation of BALTBAT was reflected in a communique signed by the Danish, Finnish, Norwegian, and Swedish Defense Ministers on May 3, 1994. On September 11, 1994, the Defense Ministers of the United Kingdom, the Nordic, and Baltic states met in Copenhagen and agreed on a Memorandum of Understanding concerning "Co-operation on the Formation of a Baltic Peacekeeping Battalion." They agreed to provide support and assistance to form BALTBAT in such areas as peacekeeping, English language, and basic military and UN unit-training.

Estonia, Latvia, and Lithuania signed an Agreement to establish and form a Joint Peacekeeping Unit on September 13, 1994. Although the battalion is unlikely to develop into a major Baltic military force, BALTBAT stands out as a practical step to coordinate Baltic defense efforts and to bring the Baltic states' defense system closer to the West. On February 8, 1995 the three presidents of the Baltic states officially opened the Baltic Battalion Training Center in Adazi, Latvia. Lithuanian President Algirdas Brazauskas said in the opening ceremony that the BALTBAT is more than a mere unit, it expresses the Baltic wish to participate with other peacekeeping battalions all over the world.

The creation of BALTBAT constitutes an important element in the security and defense policies of the Baltic states. It also conveys an important message to Moscow; that the three Baltic states are now working together to manage their security, and Western states are providing essential assistance. These recent developments can hardly be a cause for Moscow to complain. BALTBAT is too small to threaten Russia militarily; its mission involves peacekeeping, and is non-offensive. In many respects, BALTBAT sends a political message and is a very significant step towards integration in Western security structures.

Of course, Lithuania recognizes that many difficulties remain and that Lithuania's military forces have a long way to go before they can operate with their NATO counterparts. Nevertheless, it is clear that Lithuania is intent on reaching a sufficient level of interoperability with NATO through active participation in PFP.

We are aware that active PFP participation is a prerequisite for NATO membership. In this regard, the following should be noted: Lithuania introduced its Presentation Document to NATO officials during the NACC Ministerial meeting in Istanbul in June 1994 and signed its Individual Partnership Program (IPP) in November 1994, becoming the ninth partner to do so. Only the armed forces of Lithuania (and Poland) participated in all three 1994 peacekeeping exercises: in Poland (one Lithuanian detachment, on the Norwegian Sea (one light frigate), and in the Netherlands (one detachment). In addition, Lithuania was among the first to open its office at NATO Headquarters. A Lithuanian military representative has been appointed to the Partnership Coordination Cell to reside at Mons.

At present, Lithuania is preparing another IPP for 1995. On January 31, 1995 Lithuania joined the PFP Defense Planning and Review Process. Lithuania will provide the Alliance with information on its armed forces, training centers, standardization efforts, and to receive comprehensive recommendations from NATO experts. The 1995 state budget allocated 8.7 million Litas (more than $2 million) to finance the events within the PFP program. Part of this will be used to create and maintain BALTBAT, to finance activities within the PFP program, and cover peacekeeping operations in Croatia.

Lithuania regards PFP as a mechanism to reorient to Western standards. We considered this when setting cooperation priorities within the PFP program. Some of these priorities are to develop the following:

- democratic control of the military
- principles of planning and budget formation
- the concept of national security and defense doctrine
- an air defense and air control/management system
- a wide-ranging and reliable command, control, communication, and information system to able to meet the requirements of crisis management.

We also seek participation in joint land and sea exercises, development of combat skills, preparation for and participation in peacekeeping, search and rescue and humanitarian assistance exercises and operations, and assistance in the creation of a joint Baltic peacekeeping battalion, peacekeeping training.

If PFP is to have effective Partners, its priorities need to be identified to correct its deficiencies, particularly in the financial realm. A PFP fund should be established to help active partner-countries make better use of the opportunities provided by the PFP program. Reduced budgets and bilateral assistance programs are a strain and could cause difficulties for developing the PFP. In order to ensure that our transformation to Western security standards succeeds, our countries should not be left alone. As former Polish foreign minister Krzysztof Skubiszewski recently stated, the principle of international solidarity should take effect, that the rule of enlightened self-interest should come into play in view of Europe's complex interdependence.

Building on the experience of bilateral cooperation we can envisage deeper cooperation between the Alliance and partners who are more intensely engaged with NATO in practical terms and have expressed their wish for a closer long-term relationship. It is through this relationship that we can best make a positive contribution to European stability and security by bringing the West and East together. Deep bilateral cooperation should help our states convince NATO members to extend security guarantees to the East. Western societies should understand that one of NATO's new main tasks is to extend stability eastwards.

In summary, Lithuania is not a large country, nor is it a strong one. But it is a country in a very sensitive position, a country fully committed to being part of the West, and part of the new world order. For decades we have looked to the West as a model. For decades the West has encouraged us to seek freedom. Now that we have this freedom, we are committed to join the West and to build a stable democracy. We need NATO vision and help to fulfill our destiny and to be part of stable and prosperous Europe.

Endnotes

1. Conducted by a Lithuanian-British company Baltic Surveys in September 1994.

2. Letter of H.E. Mr. Algirdas Brazauskas, President of the Republic of Lithuania to Manfred Woerner, NATO Secretary General, 4 January 1994.

3. August 1994 Friedrich-Ebert-Stiftung together with Sinus (Moscow).

4. Carl Bildt, "The Baltic Litmus Test," *Foreign Affairs* (September/October 1994), p.72.

5. According to official data, there were 22,000 military "retirees" in Latvia and 10,000 in Estonia before the Russian army withdrawal from both countries.

6. Address by Algirdas Brazauskas, President of the Republic of Lithuania to the 49th Session of the General Assembly of the United Nations, New York, 30 September 1994.

Part III

Perspectives of
Soviet Union Successor States

DR. ALEXEI K. PUSHKOV

Dr. Pushkov is Director for Political and Public Affairs of the Public Russian TV (1st all-national channel) and columnist for *Moscow News*, a liberal political weekly. In 1988-1991 he served as a foreign policy adviser and speech-writer for General Secretary Mikhail Gorbachev. Since 1991 until April 1995 he was Deputy Editor-in-Chief of the *Moscow News* for foreign affairs. Dr. Pushkov is a member of the Editorial Board of *Foreign Policy Quarterly* (Washington, D.C.); Fellow of the World Economic Forum (Davos); and Member of the Council on Foreign and Defense Policies (Moscow). He contributed a number of articles on Russia's policies to *Foreign Policy, Foreign Affairs, NATO Review, The New York Times, The Christian Science Monitor, Newsday* and a number of European papers.

A View From Russia
7

Alexei K. Pushkov

The prospect of NATO enlargement to Central and Eastern Europe has become the most important and potentially explosive issue of Russia's foreign policy. It should also be regarded as the ultimate test of Russia's relationship with the West.

No other issue, such as disagreements between Moscow and Washington over the sale of a nuclear reactor or conventional armaments to Iran, the lifting of the UN sanctions against Iraq, differences over the crisis in Bosnia, or even Russia's military actions in Chechnya, can harm this relationship to the extent that NATO enlargement would. From Moscow's perspective, NATO's decision over whether or not to enlarge to the east will shape the relationship between Russia and the West for the next period of world history.

NATO's Cold War Image

Moscow's extremely nervous reaction to the prospect of NATO enlargement is closely connected with NATO's image as it was formed in Russia during the Cold War. This image did not change significantly despite the mental revolution of Gorbachev's *perestroika* and of Yeltsin's honeymoon with the West.

Paradoxically, the general picture of the West was thoroughly reconsidered by the Russian elite and general public in 1987-1991. Whereas Western countries, including the United States and Germany, were no longer regarded as Russia's enemies, NATO was still viewed as a potentially anti-Russian coalition. It was also seen as a collective enemy. The mere fact that NATO is a powerful alliance of 16 highly developed Western states, and a mechanism linking the United States to its European allies, makes it more ominous for the Russians than any single Western state, including the United States, Germany, or even Japan.

To a large extent Russia's attitude has been inherited from history. The creation of the Warsaw Pact on May 14, 1955 was portrayed as a response to NATO which had been created seven years earlier. Until the early 1990s Soviet political literature described NATO as "a military bloc of capitalist countries under American leadership, directed against USSR and other peaceful countries." NATO was seen as the centerpiece of a worldwide system of U.S. military alliances (CENTO, SEATO, ASEAN) in order to encircle the Soviet Union and "the socialist camp." At least three generations of Russians—including diplomats, journalists, military officers, and government and party officials—were brought up on this paradigm.

What made NATO look even more as the embodiment of evil was the affirmation that it was designed, among other things, to revive the German military machine, the fearsome *Wehrmacht* in order to use it against the USSR and its socialist allies in case of war. Taking into account memories from the Second World War, it was an extremely powerful argument.

Starting from the first thaw, initiated by Nikita Khrushchev in the late 1950s, fewer and fewer Soviet citizens believed that NATO would launch a military attack against the USSR or the member-states of the Warsaw Pact. However, their basic attitude towards NATO did not change. NATO was accused of trying to profit from weaknesses inside the socialist countries and of contributing to splits and tensions between them, with the goal of destroying "the socialist commonwealth." Among the strongest accusations brought against Hungarian reformers in 1956 and the initiators of the Pragues Spring in 1968-69 were revelations that they planned to leave the Warsaw Pact and join NATO. In Soviet minds, this alone, more than intentions to modify the political system or to reform the economy, was considered as the ultimate proof of the guilt of East European reformers.

During the 1970s and 1980s this image did not change, despite the rapprochement with the United States and Western Europe under Mikhail Gorbachev. One reason was the Leninist concept of two camps inside the world's bourgeoisie: a militarist, aggressive camp and a pacifist one, inclined to compromise. This concept took on new life under Khrushchev, and in the first years of detente in the early 1970s under Leonid Brezhnev.

Soviet leaders started to court representatives of the so-called "realistic and moderate forces" in the West as opposed to "aggressive and militaristic circles." NATO fell automatically in the second category. And while it was admitted that the correlation of forces inside the United States, Germany, or Great Britain could change in favor of those who called for cooperation with the Soviet Union, by definition NATO was the stronghold of the most militaristic circles in the West.

Even Mikhail Gorbachev in his 1987 book *Perestroika and New Thinking for Russia and the Whole World* condemned NATO for the split in Europe and called it "an instrument of military-political confrontation." At that time, Moscow called for the dissolution of both NATO and the Warsaw Pact, or at least of their military organizations.

At the end of the 1980s, the dominant Soviet attitude towards NATO changed to one of indifference with a tilt towards the negative. Even after the Warsaw Pact ceased to exist in 1991, NATO did not become a matter of high political or strategic concern for Soviet leaders and public opinion. Mikhail Gorbachev's concept of the common European house was for many Russians a welcome change from the Cold War division of Europe. In the new political setting, the future of the alliance appeared bleak anyway. It was widely thought NATO would lose its *raison d'etre*; it would slowly whither away and be replaced by an all-European security system.

At the same time communists and nationalists continued to affirm that NATO would benefit from the dissolution of the Warsaw Pact. They also pointed out that the Soviet Union (and later Russia) would face a new geopolitical situation in Europe which would be highly unfavorable. But these warnings were considered by many as old-fashioned and idiosyncratic. The euphoria over the end of the Cold War prevailed both in the Russian government and in the general public. After the failure of the August 1991 coup, those who adhered to the old concept of NATO as Russia's enemy (e.g., orthodox communists, KGB officers, part of the members of the military, governmental officials, and military-industrial complex) became disoriented and weakened by the Soviet Union's dissolution, and neutralized temporarily as a political force.

NATO's 1991-1993 Image

During the first two years of Yeltsin's rule, the liberal political establishment in Russia did not consider NATO to be a serious problem. Adjusting Russia's foreign policy to the requirements of rapprochement with the West seemed much more significant. The reformers' main goal was to get rid of the remnants of the communist system, to change foreign policy radically, to part with Russia's anti-Western ideological heritage, and to start integration into international economic and financial institutions (e.g., the IMF, the World Bank, and GATT). Russia largely thought that NATO would change by itself; that its main interests would become disarmament and responses to threats outside of Europe (e.g., in the Persian Gulf). Russia's geopolitical interests were virtually absent from Yeltsin's early foreign policy doctrine; the Alliance was not seen as a potential threat.

At the end of 1992, Russian Foreign Minister Andrei Kozyrev labeled the era as a romantic period in Russian foreign policy. Moscow had high hopes for Western assistance. An idealistic vision of international peace prevailed. Russia joined the North Atlantic Cooperation Council (NACC) and started to develop ties with NATO. Pro-Western liberals defined NATO as a friendly organization. In the United Nations Russia almost automatically supported all U.S. moves. In the crisis in the former Yugoslavia, Moscow backed the West's anti-Serb position. Although Russia's leaders could not make up their minds whether Moscow should ask for entry into NATO, Andrei Kozyrev's concept of strategic alliance with the West seemed to offer an answer to this question.

Predictably, such a policy did not and could not last. By the end of 1992, it became clear that the West was not ready to regard Russia, which had just emerged from 70 years of communism, as a close ally. Western powers were not eager to grant Russia a place in their own arms markets. On the contrary, Washington pressured Moscow to drop some of its intended arm deals with China and some other countries. By the summer of 1992, conservatives and communists in the Supreme Soviet sharply attacked Kozyrev's foreign policy. They insisted that this policy, inherited from the Gorbachev-Shevardnadze period, was conducive to the geopolitical strengthening of the West; to a progressive weakening of Russia on the European scene, as well as on a global scale. In the Spring of 1993, the opposition seriously questioned Moscow's stand on Yugoslavia, considering it to be pro-Western and contrary to Russia's interests.

The mood was changing in the West, too. As the political honeymoon with Russia was ending, the debates in the United States and other Alliance member-states began to focus on NATO's future. By the summer of 1993 the governments of Central and Eastern Europe started to prepare the ground for joining the Alliance; meanwhile the idea of NATO enlargement had become widely accepted in the West. In the Summer 1993 issue of *Foreign Affairs* three experts from the RAND Corporation argued for the need to enlarge NATO eastward, admitting that under certain conditions even Ukraine might become a member of the alliance, while Russia should be kept out.

President Yeltsin's famous August 26, 1993 statement in Warsaw that Eastern European countries were free to join any alliance they deemed necessary, created the pretext for bringing the NATO enlargement issue from theory into practice. Immediately after Yeltsin's visit to Warsaw, Moscow reversed its stance trying desperately to prevent enlargement. Yeltsin sent letters to the leaders of the main NATO powers making his case against the Alliance's extension to Central and Eastern Europe in the foreseeable future. His arguments reflected something more than personal or government opinion; there was a virtual consensus in Russia that NATO enlargement eastward would create conditions for the isolation of Russia, and therefore would run contrary to its national interests. Yeltsin's address to NATO leaders was based not only on advice from the alarmed Foreign Ministry, but from his Presidential Council advisors as well, and reflected a wide consensus of Russia's political class.

Zhirinovsky and Enlargement

The Russian general public remained largely indifferent to the prospects of NATO's enlargement eastward. However, it certainly contributed to the growing skepticism to the West's intentions, and a feeling that the West wanted to profit from Russia's weakness. These feelings coincided with the end of hopes for massive Western financial and economic assistance. For some, Russia did not gain, but only lost from the rapprochement with the West. This attitude contributed to some extent to the triumph of Vladimir Zhirinovsky, the ultra-nationalist leader of the Liberal-Democratic Party, in the parliamentary elections of December 1993, which gave him 24 percent of the vote.

The three main forces which determine Russia's domestic and foreign policies—political and military establishments and the bureaucracy—viewed the prospect of NATO's enlargement with deep concern; that expansion, if it took place, would be directed against Russia.

Different political forces converged on this point, too. The communists and nationalists saw in NATO's urge to enlarge a confirmation of their warnings of the United States' and other Western powers' anti-Russian intentions; according to which were plans to move NATO's troops closer to the borders of Russia.

The traditionalists—including top governmental officials, key military figures, influential members of the Yelstin administration and of the Security Council—perceived the future enlargement as a political move against Russia. They thought it would subvert Russia's security, isolate it in Europe, and result in the West taking over its former sphere of influence in Central and Eastern Europe, creating additional grounds for the American dominance in the post-Cold War world.

Radical pro-Western democrats viewed NATO enlargement not in terms of a new danger for Russia, but as a way to eliminate it from the "civilized world." They were hurt by the fact that Russia had moved decisively towards the West, but in return, the West decided not to embrace Russia, but to strengthen NATO. Some, like Foreign Minister Andrei Kozyrev, felt personally endangered, for they were accused by the conservatives of playing into the West's hands.

Finally, statist democrats (e.g., those who stand for political democracy and a strong Russian state capable of defending its national interests) both within and without the administration, stressed that NATO's enlargement, while not representing a direct danger for Russia, created conditions for its isolation and changed the geopolitical configuration of Europe in an unfavorable way to Russia. They thought that enlargement would have negative domestic repercussions, contribute to the strengthening of the communists and ultra-nationalists, help the rise of anti-Western feeling, and offer new arguments to the communist-nationalist opposition against any sort of partnership with the West.

Another argument that unified all these Russian factions, with a possible exception of a few experts and Foreign Ministry officials, was an extreme negative attitude to the idea that NATO might include Ukraine, Belarus, and the Baltic states while leaving Russia outside of the Alliance.

Partnership For Peace (PFP)

The debates over Russia's reaction to NATO expansion started in Autumn 1993 and became very tense in 1994. The debates focused around three major questions: (1) Should Russia join the Partnership for Peace? (2) What kind of Alliance relationship does Russia need? (3) What should Moscow do in response to NATO's decision to study the conditions and terms of enlargement?

Between Yeltsin's August 1993 visit to Poland and NATO's official PFP declaration in January 1994, serious debate in Russia was obscured by the fierce fight between the President and the Supreme Soviet, and then with the parliamentary elections of December 12, 1993. It was only in January 1994, when passions calmed down somewhat, that the Russian political establishment began to examine NATO's decisions and assess what they meant for Russia. The Foreign Ministry spared no efforts to make NATO leaders postpone enlargement until the indefinite future. Partially in response to those efforts, and especially to the argument that NATO's movement eastward would give an additional boost to the communists, conservatives, and ultra-nationalists, who displayed their potential force during the attempted coup on October 3-4, 1993, NATO decided to adopt a slow approach to enlargement.

The Foreign Ministry took pride in noting that NATO's rejection of immediate enlargement and the adoption of the PFP were direct results of its efforts. However, the PFP did not generate enthusiasm among the Russian political establishment. Kozyrev's boast that by making NATO adopt the PFP, that he buried NATO's plans for enlargement, was not taken seriously. It was considered as a compromise that was doomed to end and open the way for the Visegrad Four to enter NATO. Moscow considered Russia as a highly unlikely candidate for joining NATO.

While the majority of experts shared this opinion, attitudes towards PFP differed significantly. In addition to the nationalist-communist opposition, four main schools of thought appeared at this stage. The first—represented by Foreign Minister Andrei Kozyrev, top Foreign Ministry officials, and a narrow circle of experts—argued that PFP was a Russian foreign policy achievement. It stressed the West's willingness to find an arrangement acceptable both to Russia and NATO and underlined that if Moscow refused to join PFP that Russia would find itself isolated even inside the Commonwealth of Independent States (CIS), with no opportunities to influence PFP's future development. Therefore, this group called for joining the PFP and placed high hopes on interaction with NATO. Such cooperation could prevent NATO enlargement or at least postpone it well into the future.

The second school—the adversaries of Andrei Kozyrev in the parliament, the Security Council, and the Presidential Council—considered PFP an example of NATO's attitude of dictating relations with Russia. It not only argued that PFP was designed to marginalize Russia and take over its former sphere of influence in Europe, but also to weaken Russia's political and military ties with former Soviet republics. This school argued against joining PFP and for the need to keep good relations with China. Only by remaining outside the PFP, would Russia exercise "a disciplining influence and remain an independent center of power which freely determines with whom to interact and on what conditions."

The third school's main concern was that Russia in PFP would be doomed to be just one of a number of NATO partners with no special status, no say over NATO's decisions, and no freedom of maneuver. One of the participants in the State Duma debates pointed out three areas where there was a lack of clarity between NATO and Russia: in the commitments which would be taken by both sides; the mechanism of decision-making; and the forms of military and political cooperation between Russia and NATO. Despite these concerns, this group did not reject PFP. They preferred to stress the need of an "equal partnership" with NATO.

The fourth group welcomed PFP as a temporary compromise. It regarded Moscow's dialogue with Brussels as instrumental for a constructive and stable relationship between Russia and the West, and therefore stressed the political importance of Russia's participation in the PFP. It considered the adherence to PFP as the first practical step towards Russia's deeper interaction with the Alliance. At the same time, this school called for NATO to grant Russia special status or conclude a strategic agreement which would guarantee Moscow permanent participation in the activities of the Alliance without turning Russia into a member-state.

Moscow's PFP Compromise

Facing serious opposition, the Foreign Ministry changed its stance on PFP. It decided to couple Russia's signing of PFP with a specific arrangement that would single out Russia and give it a "special status."

Besides NATO's plans to enlarge, another important factor shaped Moscow's new approach towards the Alliance; differences between Russia and NATO over Bosnia. In early 1994 differences became evident when the international community looked for ways to stop the Serbian siege of Sarajevo. Russian public opinion was unsympathetic to NATO's inclination to use air strikes against the Serbs. The fact that the difference was over means and not ends helped to limit Russian irritation with the Alliance. Statements made by top Russian diplomats involved in the settlement of the Yugoslav crisis (e.g., deputy Foreign Minister Vitaly Churkin) showed their irritation. Foreign Ministry officials presented Russia's diplomatic success in making the Serbs stop the siege without the use of force, as a victory of Russia's peaceful policy over NATO's aggressive one. Somehow, they failed to mention that NATO's ultimatum to the Serbs was instrumental for Moscow's diplomatic achievements.

Russia's new coldness towards NATO made the Alliance reluctant to coordinate its actions towards Bosnia with Russia. Moscow was negative to NATO's first air-strike against the Serbs because Russia was not informed about it. Boris Yeltsin was hurt; not so much as the defender of the Serbs, but more as leader of a great power who had not been notified of a major action on which Moscow had serious doubts.

Later the Kremlin got over its initial frustration and even supported NATO air-strikes against the Serbs. But the feeling of uneasiness, compounded by NATO's steady preparations for enlargement, grew somewhat stronger when Moscow discovered that it was not a privileged partner in the contact group on Bosnia; that it had "to knock on the door" to obtain the necessary information and to make itself heard.

Initially, Moscow hoped that "strategic partnership" with the United States, and Yeltsin's personal close relations with Bill Clinton and Helmut Kohl, would suffice to make NATO postpone enlargement into the indefinite future. The protocol signed between Russia and NATO on June 22, 1994 as an addendum to the PFP agreement was definitely not enough to appease Moscow's fears and suspicions. Though the protocol recognized Russia's special status as a great power, it did not meet any enthusiasm in Moscow. In fact, it was dismissed by Kozyrev's critics as something meaningless, a mere lip-service to Russia's worries.

In order to keep the idea of cooperation with NATO alive and to sell it domestically, Andrei Kozyrev initiated talks on a special agreement on enhanced cooperation with NATO. An agreement to improve dialogue between Russia and NATO was finally reached in October 1994. It presupposed interaction in three areas: exchange of information, political consultations and cooperation in security-related areas.

The agreement marked a temporary success for Russia which had been asking for special treatment by NATO since the end of 1993. It created the possibility of Russia's cooperation with the Alliance according to the "16+1" formula. However, by the end of 1994 the general cooling of relations with the United States and the partial resurgence of old suspicions and fears towards the West neutralized whatever positive effect this agreement could have had on Russian-NATO relations, Russia's negative attitude towards NATO enlargement was building faster than diplomats could proceed with talks. Hence, Kozyrev's abrupt about-face on December 1, 1994 in Brussels. Instead of accepting the texts negotiated with NATO, the Russian Foreign Minister unexpectedly declined them under the pretext that NATO's intentions on enlargement were not clear. Only days later in Budapest, Boris Yeltsin reiterated his strong opposition to enlargement and threatened the West with a "Cold Peace."

Three Stages

One can speak of three stages in the development of Russia's relationship with NATO; each corresponding to the domestic debates over enlargement.

The first stage started in August 1993, when the issue first came into the open during Yeltsin's visit to Warsaw, until January 1994 when the PFP was adopted at the NATO summit in Brussels.

The second stage covered the period from January 1994 until December 1994. It was characterized by intensified negotiations between Russia and NATO and the development of a large Russian opposition to NATO's eastward enlargement.

The third stage started in December 1994 with Kozyrev's refusal to sign agreements on cooperation with NATO and Yeltsin's Cold Peace speech in Budapest. This stage has been characterized by the growth of tension between Russia and NATO and by the virtual consensus of Russian political elites against NATO enlargement.

This third stage coincided with the war in Chechnya. In fact, the Russian decision to resort to military force in this remote area reflected, at least partly, Yeltsin's reaction to the new distance between Russia and the West, and lost illusions about strategic partnership with Western powers. NATO's resolve to enlarge contributed to Moscow's feeling that NATO did not want to take Russia's objections seriously. Yeltsin started to have doubts whether "dear friend Bill" was really his friend. The feeling in the Kremlin was that Russia was once again on its own. Thus, NATO's declared intention to enlarge helped the decision to use force in Chechnya. Russian leaders regarded it not only as a means to solve an internal issue, but also to show Russia's growing assertiveness and strength.

The war in Chechnya changed significantly the Russian domestic scene. First, it marked the end of the shift from liberal democrats to statist bureaucrats as the main moving force of Yeltsin's rule. The struggle for influence over the Russian president was no longer between democrats and conservatives, but rather between the reformist and traditionalist factions of bureaucracy.

Second, the war in Chechnya produced a serious break between Yeltsin and all democratic parties. Since December 1994 Yeltsin had been facing strong communist-nationalist and democratic opposition, and now enjoys almost no support in the State Duma.

Third, the war strengthened conservative trends and elements in the government. In response to attacks on the government and the president the democratic circles and mass-media, the traditionalists advanced the ideology of a strong state, patriotism, and "derjavnost" (Russian for "strong power"). Those in the government and in the Yeltsin administration who were associated with the democratic movement had to change their former positions, or limit themselves to the relatively narrow field of economic reforms without interfering in political matters. The most vivid example was Foreign Minister Andrei Kozyrev who openly defected from Russia's Choice faction in the Duma when its leader, Yegor Gaidar dared to oppose Yeltsin on the war in Chechnya. Another was first vice Prime-Minister Anatoly Chubais who, in spite of his democratic credentials, preferred to keep quiet on the issue in order not to put himself in jeopardy.

The inevitably sharp, although mainly rhetorical reaction of the West to the military operation in Chechnya added to Moscow's irritation with the West. When speaking before the collegium of the Foreign Ministry on March 14, 1995, Boris Yeltsin publicly voiced this irritation.

Debates Since February 1995

When active debates over NATO enlargement resumed in February 1995 the political scenery was already significantly different from Winter-Spring 1994. The former diversity of views on NATO expansion found itself reduced to two main positions.

The first, represented by Andrei Kozyrev and his few followers in the academic community and the mass-media, started with the assumption that enlargement was unavoidable. Therefore, they argued, Russia had to accept it and start to negotiate for the best possible terms from the perspective of Russia's security.

The second, represented by the mainstream of the Russian political establishment, adopted an attitude against enlargement and remained opposed to any preliminary talks on its terms and conditions. As Yeltsin's national security assistant Yuri Baturin put it, "as to the conditions or guarantees capable of compensating the damage which NATO enlargement would inflict on the interests of Russia's national security, such conditions simply do not exist."

When Kozyrev attempted to start negotiations over the conditions of enlargement with the U.S. administration (e.g., talks between his deputy Georgi Mamedov and Deputy Secretary of State Strobe Talbott in Washington at the end of February 1995) created an uproar in the very narrow, but rather influential circle of those opposed in the presidential administration, the State Duma, the Ministry of Defense, the press, and the academic community.

The talks were regarded as backing off under NATO pressure and giving approval to the enlargement. Kozyrev's conditions—the prohibition of stationing of nuclear armaments and NATO combat troops on the territory of the future members of the Alliance in Eastern Europe—were considered meaningless. His critics argued that if the West wanted to keep a working relationship with Russia, it would refrain from stationing troops and nuclear weapons in Eastern Europe, unless there was a direct threat to its security from Russia.

Boris Yeltsin espoused the approach of Kozyrev's opponents. In a Kremlin speech before the Foreign Ministry collegium Yeltsin criticized Kozyrev for his hasty actions in negotiating the conditions of enlargement and stated that he did not approve of such talks. He reiterated his strong opposition to enlargement and suggested that Kozyrev reconsider his stand and withdraw whatever promises he had made to his Western counterparts.

Yeltsin's choice was influenced by the general shift in the Russian political establishment. Traditionalists and democrats united against NATO enlargement. In fact, a new coalition against NATO enlargement was born in Russia in December 1994. The coalition regrouped four main forces: the Yeltsin administration; the military and state bureaucracy; democratic opposition (with few exceptions); and the communist-nationalist opposition.

Paradoxically the reasons for consensus were different for each group. In the Yeltsin administration, the dominant feeling was that Russia had been very friendly towards the West and did not deserve NATO expansion. By taking the decision to enlarge, the West has betrayed the idea of partnership with Moscow.

The military and the state bureaucracy regarded enlargement as challenging Russia's security, forcing it to take military and political countermeasures. They stressed that the balance of forces in Europe is 4 to 1 in favor of NATO, and with NATO enlargement it would change even more. The democratic opposition stressed that NATO enlargement would strengthen the nationalists and communists and would weaken the democrats in Russian politics. As Vyacheslav Nikonov, a member of the State Duma put it, "all those who would like Russia to have good relations with the West, are against NATO expansion. On the contrary, all those who would like to see those relations worsen, welcome NATO enlargement."

There is a lot of truth in this. While the communist and nationalist leaders' official statements strongly attack the West for preparing NATO's eastward enlargement, they also hope that it will deal a deadly blow to Yeltsin's policy of partnership with the West, provoke an upsurge of anti-Western feeling in Russia, and contribute to their electoral success. As Vladimir Zhirinovsky once stated, "the next day after they take the decision on enlargement I will become president of Russia." A number of Russia's top-ranking military think that NATO enlargement would help to enlarge the military budget.

Consequences of NATO Enlargement

NATO enlargement will not generate a second Cold War between Russia and the West. Russia is not in a position to engage in another confrontation. At least five factors prevent Russia from setting out on this path. These include:

- its present economic weakness
- its dependence on Western financial sources and investments
- the necessity to integrate in the world economy and to become

part of international economic and financial institutions
- the desire to be part of the global decision-making (G-7)
- the weakness of its military and the absence of belligerent attitudes in the society.

Yet, it would be a big mistake to underestimate the consequences of NATO enlargement for Russian civilization, national mentality, foreign policy, and strategic posture. Those consequences fall into seven categories.

First, and historically the most important, is the deepening of the gap between Russian civilization and the West. As NATO enlargement reflects a consolidation of Western (Romano-Germanic) civilization, Russia's reaction will be to consolidate Russian civilization as distinct from the Western. NATO enlargement will leave Russia outside the Alliance and will deliver a very severe blow to Russian Westernizers and greatly benefit their opponents. The West would lose a unique opportunity to bring Russian civilization closer to itself, which is the only way to solve the West's historical task of making Russia an ally rather than a rival. Of course, Russia's progress on the road of economic reforms and creation of a working market economy will partly bridge this gap. But the decision to spread NATO over the whole of Europe will leave Russia little choice but to assert itself as a force not necessarily antagonistic but different from the Western community.

Second, NATO enlargement will result in a Russian inward reorientation. Russia will conceive its international role and national interests with less, not more respect for the interests of Western countries. After the end of the Cold War, Russia played by the rules established by the West and tried to find its role inside the Western framework. From now on, Russia will look for a much more independent role and be less constrained by a real or imagined partnership with the West. In the absence of strong strategic ties with the Western Alliance, Russia might well become a loose-canon. The effect of such reorientation remains to be seen.

Third, geopolitical consequences also will be important. If Russia considers itself cut off from Europe and the Euro-Atlantic community, it will have no choice but to strengthen its historical sphere of influence in the former Soviet Union. This will certainly mean closer economic and military cooperation with Belarus and Kazakhstan. Ukraine will be more of a problem. But here, too, Russia has powerful levers. It has especially close ties with Ukrainian enterprises, Ukrainian dependence on Russia's natural resources such as oil and gas, and 11 million ethnic Russians (over 20 percent of the population) on Ukrainian soil. One might even argue that NATO enlargement will seriously limit Ukraine's freedom to maneuver in foreign policy. Therefore, NATO enlargement will have an adverse effect on the territory of the former USSR.

Fourth, while NATO enlargement is considered a means to strengthen the security of the West and provide effective security guarantees for Central and Eastern Europe, it will seriously harm European security as a whole. Eventually NATO will have to consider the entry of the Baltic states and maybe even Ukraine into the Alliance. Russia's predictably negative reaction, as well as attempts to pressure Ukraine to prevent it from joining NATO would certainly create additional strains between Kiev and Moscow and create conditions for new tensions between Russia and the West. Any attempts to include Ukraine and the Baltic republics in NATO will result in a major crisis between Russia and the West.

Fifth, NATO enlargement will jeopardize the security structure established after the end of the Cold War. As Vladimir Lukin, head of the State Duma Committee on Foreign Affairs predicts, the decision to enlarge NATO eastward will kill the prospects for the ratification of START-2 treaty in the Russian parliament, as well as the treaty on conventional armaments in Europe and the convention on chemical weapons. According to Lukin, "NATO enlargement is the worst idea of all those that are connected with European security."

Sixth, NATO enlargement will strongly influence the balance of forces inside Russia in favor of anti-Western circles. Russia is on the eve of parliamentary elections (due to take place in December 1995) and presidential elections (June 1996). If NATO decides to expand—and there are good reason to believe it will—anti-Western and nationalist forces in Russia will use it in both electoral campaigns. (The West will be in an awkward position. While it declares support for elections and development of democracy in Russia, the West might have to back those in Russia who favor the postponement of elections and even the establishment of a dictatorial regime.)

Seventh, NATO enlargement will result in the promotion to key positions those in the Russian military who favor a strong military posture for Russia. New troops will be positioned on the western Russian border, and possibly in Belarus and the Kaliningrad area. The so-called flank restrictions will be disregarded. A new dividing line of distrust will emerge on NATO's eastern borders.

The strategy adopted by NATO which combines enlargement with a parallel enhancement of cooperation with Russia can hardly bring positive results. Russia views cooperation coupled with NATO enlargement as an obvious contradiction: either we trust each other and we cooperate, which makes enlargement meaningless; or we do not trust each other, and cooperation is rhetoric. In the words of Yuri Baturin, "the hopes for combining NATO expansion with the establishment of special partner relations with Russia are fairly weak. NATO's enlargement will sap the basis for such partnership because Russia cannot see this step as anything but unfriendly."

While the idea of a non-aggression or strategic cooperation treaty enjoyed some support in Moscow in the beginning of 1994, it is not considered very promising today. Such a treaty would have to be ratified by all NATO member-states which makes it extremely vulnerable. And if it is not accepted by at least one member-state, Russia will have to face an enlarged NATO without any strategic compensation. Finally, it may be safely predicted that after NATO decides on enlargement the negative domestic reaction in Russia will make it almost impossible for any government to conduct effective talks on Russia-NATO cooperation.

Conclusion

Today the West accuses Russia of trying to veto NATO enlargement without suggesting any alternative in the field of strengthening European security. But Russia is not in a position to veto the process. It is true that Russia does not have a clear-cut concept of relations with NATO, and that its suggestion to put more stress on the Organization on Security and Cooperation in Europe (OSCE) lacks substance. But it should be stressed that it is not Russia, but NATO which aims to change post-Cold War European security structures. Therefore it is up to NATO to make Russia a viable offer.

NATO has failed to work out a formula that satisfies Russia. Moscow has good reason to question Western leaders' sincerity. When NATO offered the Partnership For Peace to all interested countries in 1994 , Yeltsin's government saw it as an alternative to NATO enlargement which took Russia's interests into account. At the time PFP's Moscow adversaries argued that PFP was a hoax and smoke-screen for NATO's preparations for enlargement at Russia's expense. Less than a year later it turned out that they were right! NATO has stopped talking about the PFP and has been concentrating on future enlargement.

Today Moscow is faced with a take-it-or-leave-it offer: Either agree with a formal enlargement of NATO, with vague promises of cooperation and enhanced dialogue, or the enlargement will occur without Russian approval. This is hardly a means of conducting effective negotiations. NATO's suggestions to conclude a non-aggression treaty with Russia also sound hollow; such a treaty will be a mere statement that both sides do not have plans to attack each other.

NATO enlargement risks poisoning the relationship between Russia and the West for a long time. It is in the interests of both sides to prevent such an outcome. However, there seems to be little convergence in positions. While President Clinton stated that enlargement was unavoidable, President Yeltsin stressed that his negative attitude would not change. Both sides should seek rapprochement and avoid a destructive outcome.

NATO enlargement represents a huge tectonic change in European and Eurasian geopolitics. Therefore Russia, which is most affected, should be given not mere token compensation, but the following five real guarantees:

1) **Time guarantees**. NATO should make it clear that practical enlargement will not start until a remote time (e.g., the year 2000).
2) **Strategic guarantees**. NATO should not move directly to Russian borders. It should refrain from accepting Ukraine and the Baltic republics as Alliance members (offering instead PFP as compensation).
3) **Nuclear guarantees.** NATO will not station nuclear weapons in Eastern and Central Europe, including East Germany (a promise made by Kohl to Gorbachev in return for Soviet troop withdrawal from East Germany).
4) **Military guarantees.** NATO will refrain from the peacetime strategy of forward deployment of troops in Central and Eastern Europe.
5) **Treaty guarantees.** Finally, NATO should offer Russia a strategic treaty that would stipulate clearly the security-related areas of interaction between Russia and NATO.

When making such an offer and giving these guarantees, NATO should not adopt a quid pro quo attitude. If NATO did, it would undermine those in Russia who favor close relations with the West and give anti-Western forces a lot of ammunition. The West must pay a certain price for enlarging NATO against Russia's objections. If NATO does, the West risks complicating its relations with this temporarily weakened Eurasian superpower, with its huge potential, for a long time to come. And the cost of Russia's moving away from the West will tend to be much greater than the gains of NATO enlargement.

DR. IHOR KHARCHENKO

Dr. Kharchenko is the Director of Policy Analysis and Planning Department, Ministry of Foreign Affairs, Ukraine. Prior to his current appointment, he held the position of First Secretary, Head of Section at the department. From 1988 to 1992 he was the Assistant Professor, Lecturer in International Relaitons, Kyiv University. Dr. Kharchenko earned a Ph.D. in history from Kyiv University. His publications include Ukraine's Foreign Policy, Security Relations in Central and Eastern Europe, and Modern European Security Relations.

A View From Ukraine
8

Ihor Kharchenko

Ukraine's approach toward the issue of relations with NATO in general and, of late, the problem of possible NATO enlargement should include Ukraine's thinking on broader national security issues in the new international environment.

The first main outlines of Ukraine's foreign and security policy were established in July 1990 in the document "Declaration on the State Sovereignty of Ukraine" adopted by the then *Verkhovna Rada* (Parliament) of the Ukrainian SSR, under the former USSR. The Declaration claimed Ukraine's "intention to become in the future a permanently neutral state, which does not participate in military alliances and adheres to three non-nuclear principles." It also stated that Ukraine would act "as an equal partner in international relations, actively support enhancing general peace and international security, directly participate in the all-European process and European structures."

Since this document appeared more than a year before the formal disintegration of the USSR and the disbandment of the Warsaw Pact, it was regarded mainly as a declaration of intentions. Nevertheless, claims for future neutrality and nuclear-free status signified important political tendencies within the republics of the former Soviet Union (FSU), which later became the conceptual and legal framework of Ukraine's foreign policy after gaining independence.

On the one hand, Ukraine abstained from entering into the Commonwealth of Independent States (CIS) Collective Security Treaty signed in Tashkent on May 15, 1992. Ukraine cited the neutrality clause as one line of legal reasoning, along with the Reservations of the *Verkhovna Rada* to the Agreement on Establishing CIS as another. Yet another legislative provision requiring Parliament's consent for every possible case to send Ukrainian Armed Forces abroad, also influenced the government's policy on CIS security-related issues—specifically that of peace-keeping operations on FSU territory. On the other hand, in 1992 Ukraine, along with other former Warsaw Pact members and New Independent States (NIS) of the FSU, became a member of NATO's North Atlantic Cooperation Council (NACC) and showed great interest in promoting NACC activities.

Ukraine's appearance in the so-called "security vacuum," brought Ukraine's foreign policies closer to the concept of common European security and stability and to future participation in an all-European security system. During 1992-93 the President and Foreign Minister of Ukraine publicly stated that the ultimate goal of Ukraine was to be in European structures.

Ukraine's Foreign Policy Concept approved by the Parliament on July 2, 1993 transcended the "neutrality clause" and sorted out the contradiction between neutrality and cooperation with NATO in the NACC framework, as well as with other international structures. The Concept noted that Ukraine "stands for the creation of comprehensive international system of universal and all-European security and considers the participation in them as the fundamental component of her national security." It also noted that "due to the elimination of bloc confrontation in Europe, the issue of creating all-European security structure on the basis of existing international institutions such as CSCE, NACC, NATO, WEU becomes the issue of prior significance. Ukraine's direct and full membership in such a structure will ensure the relevant external assurances of her national security. Taking into account the crucial transformations following the disintegration of the USSR, and which shaped Ukraine's geopolitical situation, her before stated intention of becoming a neutral, non-bloc state should be adapted to new circumstances. Ukraine's intent cannot be construed as an obstacle to her full-scale participation in the all-European security structure."

The Parliament approved the Military Doctrine of Ukraine in mid-October 1993. It included the main parameters of the Foreign Policy Concept and the claim of Ukraine's adherence to non-bloc country status. Thus the national legal and political framework had been established for Ukraine's international security policies.

Ukraine became one of the most outspoken champions of the development of closer political and military relations between former Cold War adversaries and displaying great interest in the activities of the NACC. In fact, Ukraine viewed NATO's creation of a cooperation forum on security issues as an extremely important step in enhancing all-European stability and security. Politically extending NATO's security dialogue to the partners "out-of-area" meant *de facto* expansion of the Alliance's activities and contributed significantly to the development of the "interlocking institutions." It was designed to fill the security vacuum in the new Europe and to address the emerging hierarchy of existing European security institutions.

Ukraine's policy during the first years of NACC's existence was directed at its consolidation and finding practical means for the proper "division of powers and responsibilities" between European security institutions in the new historical circumstances. Ukraine's Foreign Policy Concept sets the principle of indivisibility of security as the highest priority in international endeavors. Being strategically located in one of the most vulnerable regions of Europe, Ukraine regards this formula to be the principal issue in contemporary politics.

Following this line, in 1993 Ukraine proposed to seek all possible solutions, including potential regional and sub-regional levels, strengthening security confidence in Europe, and creating a stability and security zone in Central and Eastern Europe (CEE). This could serve as a political and psychological filling of the regional "security vacuum" and linking of Western structures and Russia. That idea shared elements with Poland's President Walesa's concept of NATO-bis, and was mainly directed at avoiding new dividing lines in Europe and strengthening Central and East European regional confidence. The accent on CEE regional efforts later became a part of the French/European Union (EU)'s proposal of a European Stability Pact.

With the growth of CEE cooperation partners' mounting criticism of the "looseness" of the NACC framework and ambiguity about its future, the issue of the Alliance's formal enlargement came to the fore. This focused the European security discussion on the issue of NATO's future either as a collective defense or collective security structure.

Ukraine's concentrated on maintaining a stable European security architecture while preserving the political momentum to build a united Europe on the principles of indivisibility of security. On the issue of possible NATO enlargement, Ukraine stressed throughout 1993-1994 that its principal goal was to adequately safeguard the nation's vital security interests vis-a-vis the realities of the new security environment that emerged after the collapse of the Warsaw Pact and dissolution of the FSU.

One related issue was the nuclear powers' security guarantees for Ukraine in connection with the elimination of nuclear weapons located on her territory. Throughout 1992-1994 Ukraine had been insistent on receiving such a guarantee as a prerequisite for the final decision to eliminate nuclear weapons and accede to the Non-Proliferation Treaty (NPT). Ukraine used the North Atlantic Cooperation Council to express her concerns on the issue and succeeded in developing NACC consensus on this problem. As a result, several ministerial NACC statements supported Ukraine's position to seek security guarantees in return for non-nuclear-weapon state status. The roles of the United States as well as of Central and East European NACC partners were important. They openly expressed understanding and support for Ukrainian concerns.

In the course of debates during 1992-1994 on the issue of NATO's future with respect to Ukraine and her immediate western neighbors that are seeking Alliance membership, both sides expressed similar views on the role of the Alliance. The differences in the approaches of Ukraine and CEE applicants for NATO membership lie not in political philosophy but rather in practicalities, formalities, and geographic realities. Ukraine remains critical of the geographically and politically restricted "6+3" (Visegrad states, Romania, Bulgaria, and the Baltic states) formula of Western European Union (WEU) cooperation with post-communist eastern democracies. Ukraine considers this formula to be rather "exclusive," contrary to the wider dimension of NACC and PFP cooperation framework.

Pursuing the policy of "indivisibility of security," Ukraine expressed open support to the principle of "inclusiveness and not exclusiveness" which had been taken as the foundation of the Partnership for Peace program proposed by the United States and NATO. Ukraine became one of the first signatories to the PFP Framework Document and remains the champion of furthering cooperation in the PFP framework, viewing the program as the very important practical exercise of former adversaries' cooperation "on the ground." Extremely significant is the possibility of direct military-to-military collaboration, including NATO's and former Warsaw Pact members' participation in military field exercises, which helps to eliminate the "enemy" mentality. For Ukraine, this particular point was among the principal, positive aspects of PFP.

Ukraine's stance towards PFP also involves internal and external political aspects of her national security doctrine and are directly connected with its views on enlargement. In Ukraine's fundamental legislative documents is a "neutrality clause" which affects Ukraine's participation in PFP.

There were some comments in the public debate in Ukraine on whether this neutrality clause should prevent the country from joining any multilateral forms of security cooperation, PFP included. PFP's "inclusiveness" and the participation of traditional European "neutrals" (e.g., Sweden, Finland, Austria)—who joined PFP, but are remaining cautious of joining NATO—are the most important to Ukraine's approach to this issue. Ukraine's unpoliticized and "low profile" course in establishing formal relations with NATO through NACC and PFP did not cause the strong political debate that it did in Russia. The "neutrality clause" and the highly-profiled "nuclear" issue of acquiring security guarantees in return for signing the NPT overshadowed public thought concerning NATO enlargement and the PFP.

Official Policy on NATO Enlargement

Ukraine's official approach to the issue of NATO enlargement may be summarized by the following. First, Ukraine has never renounced the idea of possible NATO enlargement as an option for its future development. NATO's enlargement primarily lies within the scope of responsibilities of NATO and the applicant country. No one can exercise a "veto" over nations trying to decide on whether or not to join any international organization. This is a normal and recognized principle of interstate behavior and of international law.

Second, the "no-veto" principle must not be exercised without taking into consideration the security concerns of other interested parties whose stability and security may be affected. This goes directly to the practical implementation of Ukraine's principle of "indivisibility of security" in a united Europe. Ukraine is firmly committed to promote the building of a comprehensive and "inclusive" all-European security structure with adequate security assurances for every participant so that Europe will not be divided again into military-political blocs. Ukraine considers the renovation of old security divisions along geographic lines to be the development most detrimental to the cause of building a new undivided Europe.

Third, European security is mainly characterized by the parallel existence of NATO and the Tashkent collective security treaty—the CIS states. The modalities and scope of these two structures, as well as their possible cooperation, are not very clear. Nonetheless, it is obvious that Russia, the leading power of the Tashkent treaty, maintains a very negative stance on the issue of NATO enlargement to the east. It has also often been argued that the Tashkent treaty structure, for formal and political reasons, cannot be regarded as a genuine collective security institution.

Under such circumstances, an important part of NIS public opinion equates the parallel institutions with the "Cold War" period. Ukraine's approach is to avoid any situation in which such parallels may be drawn. Ukraine is also greatly concerned about the possibility of appearing to be a "buffer state" between an enlarged NATO and unstable Tashkent treaty structure.

Fourth, Ukraine considers that Central and Eastern Europe's (the region to which Ukraine organically and historically belongs) clear-cut and persistent desire to quickly join NATO must force the Alliance to reconsider its role in modern Europe. It must widen the scope of its evolution from a classic-type collective defense system to a collective security institution, becoming the relevant and efficient nucleus of a future all-European security system. Ukraine sees full-scale participation in such a system as the necessary and natural assurance of her national security.

Fifth, Ukraine does not reject the idea of possible NATO enlargement and sees this process as neither speedy nor momentous. The realities of modern European security development and Ukraine's natural security concerns demand a certain unspecified period of time during which the question of NATO enlargement should not focus on two main issues: the "who" and "when." This time period is needed for two reasons:

1)   to prevent the overburdening of the unstable political situation in NIS, who are attempting to build open democratic societies; and
2)   to allow for the evolution of consensus on NATO's new role as the efficient mechanism for creating an all-European security system in cooperation with other existing structures.

Ukraine also considers that during this period, that special attention should be given to effective and deep implementation of the Partnership for Peace program, which creates substantial opportunities for all interested countries (both partners and non-partners) to develop practical cooperation with the Alliance.

Ukraine's specific views on enlargement are influenced by the issues of Russia-NATO and Ukraine-NATO relationships. Though they seem to have many similarities, they do vary in some very important aspects.

Ukraine is interested in developing normal and fruitful relations between NATO and Russia, including working out specific formal modalities of such relationships. Ukraine believes that it is impossible and even hazardous to consider that a new European security structure can be created without Russia. The "indivisibility of security" principle is crucial in this regard. There must be no attempt to create a European security architecture that creates a feeling of "isolation" in any country, specifically in Russia, which has a unique geopolitical and security posture. Ukraine is also confident of the need to exclude "zones of influence" while seeking a durable formal relationship between NATO and Russia.

Ukraine, which also possesses a significant geopolitical posture in Europe, considers it necessary to ensure the scope of her relations with the Alliance. This approach is based on the assumption that both the NATO-Ukraine relationship and NATO-Russia relationship are important to the process of NATO's enlargement. NATO enlargement directly concerns the basic security interests of Ukraine: a country of 52 million people, with one of the largest military potentials on the continent. While Ukraine has not applied for NATO membership, Ukraine deems it necessary to work out the modalities of a *special relationship* with the Alliance, beyond the framework of PFP and NACC. Developing a NATO-Ukraine "special relationship," should be parallel with the NATO-Russia dialogue, but the two processes should not be confused.

Ukraine, like Russia, is a part of the NACC, a partner in PFP, and it already has a formalized relationship with NATO, including in the military sphere. But Ukraine, unlike Russia does not have formalized military ties with the CIS Tashkent collective security arrangement. In addition, NIS public opinion, especially in Russia, but to some extent also in Ukraine, still thinks of NATO as an "aggressive" structure of the Cold War period.

Under such circumstances, it is important to create the external and internal prerequisites for Ukraine and Russia to feel comfortable with future decisions on enlargement. The implementation of the "inclusiveness" principle is one of the most pressing issues in the whole enlargement debate. Ukraine's position here is very clear. When making the enlargement decision, the environment must be "ripe" not only in the relationship of NATO- applicant countries, but also in the regions and countries directly interested and involved.

Ukraine's position on this is different from Russia's. Russia, as a global power, has its own very specific security interests. Ukraine is not a global power and is mainly preoccupied with the need to create a stable and friendly external environment to allow the country to proceed with the task of creating an open democratic European society with a market economy. In this context Ukraine's priority is to develop closer and mutually beneficial ties with Russia and her immediate western (and, as yet, non-NATO) neighbors, as well as to gradually extend relations with the West.

To achieve these ends Ukraine conducts a two-part foreign policy. To the east Ukraine engages in bilateral dialogue with Russia and other NIS, as well as with the CIS. To the immediate west, Ukraine's activities are mainly bilateral. As for general relations with the West, Ukraine combines both bilateral and multilateral efforts, but feels limited to the latter. In fact, NACC is Ukraine's *only* structure for security dialogue. But NACC, a NATO subsidiary, provides a very limited scope for addressing Ukraine's basic security interests. The PFP is a very important and quite logical extension of NACC, but it can not be regarded as an international security structure.

Keeping in mind Ukraine's "neutrality clause" and its specific geopolitical location, it is extremely important for all-European stability and security that Ukraine acts as a link between Central Europe and Russia. Balancing Ukraine's relationships with the West and the East is also important. An uncontroversial solution for safeguarding this specific role for Ukraine, which has already obtained security guarantees of five Western and Eastern nuclear countries, is to work out a closer formal relationship with NATO in the context of a "special relations" formula while preserving an open and close special relationship with Russia.

Although there remain traces of the communist ideological indoctrination of NATO's so-called "aggressiveness" and "enmity" in public and political minds in Ukraine and Russia, views on NATO differ. Russia witnessed a heated political debate on the issue of whether to join PFP in the first half of 1994; this was not the case for Ukraine. While Russia canceled the planned joint military exercise with U.S. units on Russian territory due to strong political opposition; Ukraine's military units have already participated in PFP military exercises in Poland, the Netherlands, and a joint United States-Ukrainian exercise in Ukraine in May 1995. One reason for the difference is that unlike Russia, Ukraine pursued a rather "low profile" policy on these issues, and preferred to seek practical cooperation.

These differences also influence what may be achieved in the NATO-Ukraine and NATO-Russia dialogues.Ukraine does not want the possible outcome in the current NATO-Russia negotiations to be linked to the prospects of the Ukraine-NATO relationship, for these two cases are different. The issue is quite complex because of the very significance of the Ukraine-Russia relationship.

The prospects of reaching a closer Ukraine-NATO tie seems to be more feasible now, since the two sides do not have outstanding issues on their agenda. Russia's approach on enlargement presently impedes prospects for finding a quick mutually acceptable solution. In the end, however, the outcome of NATO-Russia negotiations, will influence not only the whole process within the Alliance, but also the modalities of the Ukraine-NATO future relationship. The reasons for this are simply the characteristics of Ukrainian-Russian relations and the difference between Ukraine-CIS and Russia-CIS stances.

The prospects of achieving a consensus on ultimate Russian-NATO and Ukrainian-NATO formal relationships remain unclear. Part of this lack of clarity can be traced to the unknown nature of possible "compromise" in the NATO-Russian dialogue. Many important issues of European security are within the scope of this "enlargement-related" Alliance and Russian Federation dialogue. And they are matters of high priority from Ukraine's perspective.

A public debate is now under way in Central and East Europe— Ukraine included—and some NIS on the parameters of the so-called "Grand Compromise" between the Alliance and Russia. Of the several proposed "package deal" options being discussed, some fall into the scope of Ukraine's concerns.

Ukraine has been consistent in her view that any possible "spheres of influence" deal is absolutely irrelevant in today's Europe. Also any attempts to create the image that different "zones of responsibility" may exist in Europe are very dangerous. In particular, this refers to the so-called "specific responsibility of Russia" on the territory of the former Soviet Union.

This issue is ideologically and propagandistically loaded; and it is important to note that these arguments do influence public opinion in post-communist societies, which experienced totalitarian rule for decades. Ukraine, being the biggest and the closest neighbor of the Russian Federation and sharing a historic relationship, is the most exemplary case of the complexity of this problem.

Disruption of ties between Russia and Ukraine is both unwise and unrealistic. Adding an "outer" security element to the complicated Ukraine-Russia bilateral dialogue only complicates this dialogue, even if the real policy is balanced and well-designed. Thus, in the context of the NATO enlargement debate, avoiding the possibility of "greater Russian influence" in the so-called "near abroad" becomes a very important task and, in fact, one of the most challenging issues for Ukraine.

Against this background, it is necessary to facilitate non-confrontational "parallelism" in the Russia-NATO and Ukraine-NATO dialogues on the modalities of their future formal relationships. The PFP does provide a sufficient and proper mechanism to achieve these ends, and it should be exploited. The basic issue, though, is Russia's attitude towards PFP. After agreeing to take part in the program in June 1994, Russia then took a different stance regarding the prospects of active participation. Ukraine supported Russia's active participation in the PFP, considering this as one of the important new links in the emerging all-European security system. Ukraine continues to call for broader cooperation of Russia within the PFP framework, and supports the widening of the list of participants.

In the end, NATO's relationship with Ukraine and Russia will inevitably reveal significant differences. The relationship should not be approached in terms of who will come "closer" to the Alliance in developing formal ties. Essentially the difference is not just due to geopolitics. Russia is a part of the CIS collective security arrangement, and Ukraine is not. Russia is a nuclear power, and Ukraine is completing implementation of START-I, approaching *de-facto* non-nuclear status. Ukraine and Russia are very special partners not only within the CIS, but also in historic terms. Finally, Russia and Ukraine still have some important bilateral issues with internal and external security ramifications (e.g., the Black Sea Fleet) to resolve.

All these realities lead to a conclusion that the likely outcome of NATO's relationships with Ukraine and Russia will be different. An additional important element is the fact that the two countries have different views on the CIS relationship to PFP and on the issue of NATO enlargement. What may be understood as seeking consensus among the members of the Tashkent Treaty, does not necessarily coincide with the political framework and modalities of the PFP Program and the proposed individual character of the "why and how" to enlarge, as well as the future "who and when" discussion of enlargement. Ukraine's point of view is based on the "indivisibility of security" principle, and on the principles of inclusiveness, openness, and transparency.

The final result of the Ukraine-NATO dialogue is not very clear, since the NATO study of how to enlarge is continuing. Nevertheless, Ukraine is definitely interested in a relationship with NATO that embraces both regular political and close practical military ties. Ukraine also is definitely interested in a specific format for NATO-Ukraine security consultations on a continual basis, as well as direct participation in some Alliance bodies dealing with specific activities.

For the time being, Ukraine will not seek Article 5 guarantees. At the same time, it seeks to create a formal Ukraine-NATO relationship that embraces both the "16+1" framework and wider multilateral formulae. Ukraine wants to keep its future options open and remain generally connected to the evolving new European security architecture. Finally, Ukraine does not want any country to infringe on its security interests. This last premise is definitely the most controversial and complex one, specifically in the context of the Russian-NATO dialogue.

In the long-term, deliberations over NATO enlargement should lead, together with the OSCE discussion of a security model for the 21st century, to a more comprehensive idea of what the future European security architecture should look like. Ukraine champions a balanced, evolutionary, and step-by-step approach to possible future NATO enlargement, and speaks consistently for concentrating united efforts to create a new security system for Greater Europe that will embrace all interested countries, without any exceptions, in the trans-Atlantic region.

Existing security institutions—notably OSCE, NATO, and WEU—should serve as nuclei of this future system. The problem now lies in the essence and modalities of "interlocking" these institutions without triggering the potentially dangerous issues of hierarchy and "chain of command." A new European consensus security concept should arise. Time is pressing.

MR. ANATOL MAISENIA

Mr. Maisenia is President, East-West National Centre for Strategic Initiatives. Prior to his current appointment, he was a Columnist in the "Narodnaja Gazzetta" newpaper in Minsk. From 1989 to 1990, Mr. Maisenia was Special Correspondent, New Program, USSR TV. He graduated from the Minsk Institute for Foreign Languages and did post graduate studies at the Institute of Philosophy and Law, Academy of Sciences of Belarus. He earned a Ph.D degree based on a dissertation on American Politics.

A View From Belarus
9

Anatol Maisenia

During the second part of the 1980s, deep changes took place in the world. The post-Cold War world underwent radical changes before our very eyes. The systemic disease that had been undermining for a long time the forces of the communist nations and regimes finally led to their disappearance, the break-up of their military-political Warsaw Treaty Organization, and the collapse of the USSR, the stronghold of world communism.

These processes, which were accompanied by outbursts of uncontrolled energy, are still in progress in Europe. The transitional period from non-democratic, authoritarian, super-centralized orders to democracies and market economies entails such contradictory phenomena as the partial loss of control of social processes and a reinforcement of military-political instability. This epoch creates new challenges for Europe.

The former security system, based on the opposition between blocs and the policy of nuclear deterrence and "balance of fear," was actually distorted. It has been razed to the ground and will not be restored.

The outline of a new system is beginning to take shape. The key principle—"to strive for peace and prepare for war"—of the Cold War security system has changed. Today, the system of European security is filled with mutual activity aiming to prevent or to handle conflict situations on the continent, instead of preparing for military conflicts with a defined enemy.

Threats To Security

Instead of the stability and predictability of the former communist nations we have instability and unpredictability. The politicians who presently hold power lack understanding of the "rules of the game" and

155

their rhetoric is often represented by militant nationalism. These changes are especially vivid in some states newly formed from the ruins of the USSR. And this seems to be a major threat to Europe.

The uncontrolled, spontaneous break-up of the Soviet Union led to a rather uncivilized division of arms and military equipment. Division was based on a formal territorial principle (i.e., wherever arms and equipment were located at the time of the USSR's collapse). This turned out to be a source of conflict itself.

The threat to security and stability in Europe was also burdened by uncertainty about the fate of nuclear arms located on the territories of four independent states: Russia, Ukraine, Kazakhstan, and Belarus. This was dramatically demonstrated by the conflict between Russia and Ukraine on the Black Sea Fleet issue, their notorious rivalry on controlling nuclear arms, and attempts to retain their property on the territorial principle. These were just echoes of the spontaneous disintegration of the USSR.

The degeneration of national liberation and democratic movements into wild nationalism in some republics of the former USSR has nothing to do with democracy and is a serious cause of instability and a source of inter-ethnic conflicts. Nationalism always tries to create an "enemy image" to justify its existence. Nationalism is irrational, and when combined with power and nuclear ambitions becomes an extremely flammable mixture.

Most often Russia is portrayed as such an "enemy" or an "evil empire." This results not only from distorted nationalist perspectives, it also results from Russian policies toward neighboring states.

Anti-Russian attitudes are reinforced in some of Russia's neighboring countries as a reaction to Russian attempts to direct economic policy in those countries. Russia operates from the position of "economic egoism" and remains aloof from the deep energy and financial crisis that has enveloped the former republics. This crisis remains a basic factor of instability.

Despite the fact that many newly independent states (NIS) retain the psychology and traditions of the Soviet Army, under the present conditions of economic discord, civil controls over the armed forces are being reduced. Acute technical problems and inability to provide for the welfare of national armed forces are other significant risks. The recent events of the Black Sea Fleet serve as an illustration of this. States in economic disarray should not be in control of nuclear arms.

Stability is also undermined by the ghosts of theocratic regimes in the CIS's southern borders, as well as by the reinforcement of religious fanaticism in Central Asian republics. In this region, living standards have declined and mass consciousness has developed a "neurotic reaction" to the burden of material existence. All this makes for greater instability.

Though Russia is being called on to serve as a stronghold of stability and security all around the former USSR, it is unable to carry out this role objectively. Russia itself is going through the most acute internal disorder; the system is experiencing its own crisis of power. Thus, Russia has become a major center of instability and challenge to European security.

Constructing a New European Security System

The interests of survival require the West to adequately answer threats to stability. This is a condition of great importance to the security and well-being of Europe. Also, successful reforms to create market conditions in the NIS will contribute to military-political stability. Western countries spent from 3 to 5 per cent of their GNP on the arms race. They must understand that the creation of an efficient system of European security, by overcoming the crisis in Eastern European nations, will also require considerable expense. Now they must provide assistance in place of weapons purchases.

The shortest way to create a secure and stable Europe lies through the opening of a European perspective for the NIS and their inclusion in the common European economic space (e.g., process of "Euro-construction"). I speak not only about material, technical, and consulting assistance, but also an active exploration of eastern markets and opening of western markets to CIS goods. Finally this requires working out a new European security architecture and institutionalizing it.

The aim is to create a multiple-level system of collective security and to ensure efficient interaction of its elements. The North Atlantic Cooperation Council (NACC) and the Helsinki Process must be given new impetus. In the framework of the Helsinki Process, it might be advisable to consider establishing a European Security Council which would reflect common European interests and would ensure their organic link with the Euro-Atlantic countries.

Creating a military-political organization is required to ensure that the European Security Council's resolutions are carried out. Also the equal participation of Western, Central, and Eastern European nations seems to be an indispensable condition for such an organization as guarantor of security and stability in Europe.

The same condition applies to NATO which is attempting to revalidate its role in the post-Cold War world. NATO is stepping beyond its traditional environment. But its new role can be realized only when the NATO structure and organization is widened to include Russia and other newly independent states in its activities. This is an indispensable condition. If it does not, enlargement of NATO's involvement in Europe might become destructive and an element of instability.

In the process of constructing a new system of European security, one should not underestimate the role of the "Atlantic factor" and, of course, its main body; the United States. Recognizing the United States' interest in Europe and its specific responsibility for maintaining peace and stability on the planet, it is necessary to define the admissible limits and spheres of the American involvement in European affairs. First, it is necessary to avoid political interventionism in the areas that are traditionally beyond the American "sphere of influence." This is absolutely relevant to the geopolitical area of the former Soviet Union. Otherwise, collisions of national interests and new sources of tension will be inevitable.

In these regions it seems to be more advisable to realize American political initiatives through supranational mechanisms and institutions, not unilaterally. In this connection, I would like to draw attention to a recent statement of former U.S. Defense Secretary, Les Aspin, regarding the readiness of the United States to act as a go-between in Ukrainian-Russian negotiations on nuclear weapons and disarmament controls. The same might be said about the attempts to hand over the main peace-making role in the Caucuses to the United States.

Recognizing U.S. limitations is not based on anti-American attitudes; they are just a reflection of geopolitical realities. These realities also suggest the specific need to update and increase the coordinating role of supranational institutions as well as strengthening their integration function in European affairs. Simultaneously, the process of creating new supranational organizations and diversifying regional interstate associations is taking place.

The future architecture of European security will need to comprise a complex multi-level configuration which will have "vertical" and "horizontal" dimensions. The horizontal section of the new European security system gives a picture of the crossing spheres of influence and interaction of different regional organizations. And herein lies its principal difference from the post-war bipolar structure of Europe and the world.

If we accept this notion then the idea of the complete neutrality of Belarus proclaimed in the Declaration of Independence makes no sense. It becomes synonymous with voluntary self-isolation and leads to the injury of Belarus' national interests.

A complicated "holographic" perception of future European security gives Belarus the opportunity to participate in creating such regional associations as the Baltic and Black Sea Union, and associate with the states from the "Visegrad group," as well as "NATO-bis" or "Warsaw Pact" suggested by Polish President Lech Walesa. According to Walesa this cooperation and security "NATO-bis" union would include Poland, Hungary, the Czech Republic, Slovakia, Moldova, Ukraine, Romania, the Baltic states, and Belarus. The idea of "NATO-bis" reflects the traditional economic and political attraction of former Warsaw Treaty-partners united in a common geopolitical space. And as observers have noted, this is a reaction to the unwillingness of the West to open up its markets and NATO doors to eastern European countries.

Even a superficial analysis of this idea confirms its right to exist. However, I can only caution the inspirers of this project against any attempts to play the "threat from the East" card. If the NATO-bis (or "Warsaw Pact") or the Baltic and Black Sea Union acquires an anti-Russian grounding, it could lead to explosions over all of Europe.

At the moment, there are no serious reasons for anxiety except some provocative statements. It is quite inexplicable that the reaction of the semi-official Russian press to the "Warsaw Pact" is rather rigid. This involves Russia's steady hostility to the idea of creating a belt of non-nuclear states of the Baltic and Black Sea region. It is a natural right of every sovereign state to get together with whatever state it chooses for the sake of national security.

NATO's January 1994 Brussels Summit commenced a new stage in NATO history and finally reconsidered the role and the place of this military-political organization in the changed world. Out of the Cold War and bloc opposition, NATO came out the winner having buried its long-term enemy, the Warsaw Treaty Organization, under the fragments of communism. But NATO was unable to continue in the old way.

The agenda for modern policy—stability and world order through mutual cooperation—requires a fundamentally new architecture for European and global security. The major problem here is to work out a proper correlation between NATO and other key institutions (e.g., the UN, EC, CSCE, and WEU) and determine their relevant position in the global security system.

In discussions held immediately before the NATO Brussels Summit it was clear that NATO circles were developing a sense of political realism. Some East European countries proposed joining NATO directly. Poland played the first violin in this company. In the final days before the Summit, the East Europeans united in a so-called club of NATO candidates. They engaged in decisive actions and imposed great pressure on the NATO leadership and heads of member-states.

In late December 1994, Polish President Lech Walesa stated in a *Washington Post* interview that "the Russian bear cannot be tamed" adding that if the West did not listen to Polish arguments, that the devils will awaken and something like Yugoslavia may happen. Similar statements were also made by Czech and Hungarian leaders. On the very eve of the New Year, Lithuania, also frightened by the results of Russia's parliamentary elections, knocked on NATO's doors. The "Zhirinovsky factor" and the increase in pro-empire and ultra-nationalist attitudes in Russia heightened East European concerns.

The increase of pro-NATO attitudes in Eastern Europe was also encouraged by Russia's lack of clarity on this issue. Boris Yeltsin actually approved Central Europe's endeavors to join NATO during his August 1993 visit to Warsaw. While it is hard to say whether it was one more "improvisation" of the Russian president, in fact, several weeks later the official Moscow position was highly critical of NATO's plans to enlarge. The most rigid statement was made by Boris Yeltsin's press-secretary in reference to Lithuania.

In the end, the West held out against the Central and Eastern European pressure to join. NATO did not decide to enlarge NATO's zone eastward. Does that mean that the West remained deaf to Lech Walesa's warnings about the "war devils" dozing in Russia and to other East European arguments? Does that mean that NATO effaced itself under Kremlin pressure? Of course not! Choosing between bad and worse alternatives, the leaders of the North Atlantic Treaty stuck to a more cautious and considered position. We should particularly note that American and French efforts contributed the most to NATO's success.

NATO Arguments Leading to Partnership For Peace

First, NATO leaders became aware that the consequence of widening the NATO membership list would not promote European and global security, but rather undermine it. Since quantity did not turn into quality, the White House put forward the more attractive idea of "Partnership For Peace" (PFP).

PFP gradually spreads out NATO's influence as a global military-political organization to the all of Central and East Europe, and the former Soviet Union (FSU). This idea does not bring back to life the ghosts of "bloc policy" and the "cordon sanitaire," but it creates equal possibilities and conditions for all ex-members of the Warsaw Treaty to qualify. And what is the most important, it involves Russia in the partnership.

Second, the decision reinforced the process of European integration. Since the United States is apparently unwilling to participate in ground operations in European conflicts (e.g., in Yugoslavia), there is a need to redistribute roles between NATO and the Western European Union (WEU). The WEU will take the main responsibility for continental security to prevent and solve conflict situations in Europe. It seems logical in the context of Euro-construction that the WEU will assume this role since it is an instrument of the European Union.

That is why—as distinct from entering into NATO—there is no objection to the proposal that East European countries join the WEU as associate members. The more so since they are full members of the Council of Europe.

Third, even if NATO leaders have no intention to create a "cordon sanitaire" in Central Europe, many things could happen despite their intentions. Moreover, there could develop an institutional security because military-political organizations (NATO included) live under their own rules. For this reason, Russia's reaction is quite natural. NATO's coming close to its borders is understood as a threat to Russian security.

Fourth, the West must understand that the striving of Poland, Hungary, the Czech Republic, Romania, and other Central and East European states for NATO membership is also motivated by economic ambitions. In this way, these states are trying to break into Western markets.

Finally, one more important reason is that Russia remains a powerful military nation and historically has interests in Eastern Europe and the

Baltic states. In addition, we should also take into account the force of anti-NATO attitudes in Russian society. The acceptance of new members in NATO from Eastern Europe would definitely cause a wave of imperial ambitions, which might lead to an uncontrolled collapse of Russia's political system and chaos with nuclear weapons. That is the time when the "war devils" can wake up.

It is more important to the West to preserve Russia's readiness for cooperation and movement toward reforms than give instant security guarantees to the Central and East European states. And this position ought to be in effect until any direct threat to the continent emerges from Moscow. But if such a case arose, the West will know what to do. Senator Sam Nunn has noted that if pro-empire forces in Russia are victorious, formation of an anti-Russian coalition will be inevitable. In that case, Russia will be to blame for having a new "cordon sanitaire" built.

Impact of NATO Enlargement on Belarus

If Poland had been accepted into the Alliance, it would have brought NATO to Belarus' borders. That would have presented Belaurus with a tough choice; it most likely would have resulted in close alliance with Russia in common opposition to the West. Fortunately, events took a different course, and Belarus got a chance to foster cooperation with both the West and the East.

Independent Belarus is located right between two power centers—a highly integrated Western Europe and Russia. Due to its geopolitical position, Belarus must create two foreign policy vectors to gradually level the legacy of imbalance. This process of overcoming its excessive economic and political dependence on Russia will take many years.

Russia must be encouraged to leave behind any jealousy and partiality. Belarus must also be encouraged to pursue its national interests. In fact, Eurasian Russia itself has the same active foreign policy course as Belarus. It needs to support and cement its membership in different regional unions and associations. In any case, Russia will remain a strategic ally and partner of Belarus.

Proceeding from the placement of existing forces in Europe, the integration of the CIS states, and the outlined paradigm of European security, the place and the role of Belarus is in the CIS. There is no alternative to such a military-political union. Though Belarus must define the principles of its participation and limits of involvement due to its own national interests. That is an inalienable right.

The main choice for Europe today lies between restoring the post-war bloc structure or creating a new flexible multi-level system of security and cooperation. Belarus' earlier political leaders realized that and abandoned their foolish illusions of prosperity in neutrality.

Part IV

How NATO Must Change

MR. HANS JOCHEN PETERS

Mr. Peters is the Head, Central and Eastern Europe and Liaison Section, Political Affairs Division, NATO International Staff. Before his current assignment, he held the position of Foreign Policy Advisor to Minister President of the Land Schleswig-Holstein from 1989 to 1991. From 1987 to 1989, he was the Speechwriter for Foreign Minister Genscher and from 1984 to 1987 Mr. Peters was a member of Foreign Ministry Policy Planning Staff. From 1975 to 1981, Mr. Peters was Federal Chancellery, Bonn (Deputy Head, Eastern Europe Section, and later Private Secretary to Chancellor Schmidt and Deputy Head of his Private Office. Mr. Peters joined the German Foreign Service in 1970 and was assigned abroad in Moscow, USSR from 1973 to 1975 and Montevideo, Uruguay from 1981 to 1984. He studied Slavic Languages, History, Political Science, and Philosophy at the University of Tubingen. He also attended the University of Kiel.

The Political Dimension
10

Hans Jochen Peters

The enlargement of NATO will be the most significant decision the organization has had to take since the dual track decision of 1979. And like the decision of 1979, it may entail long-range consequences, many of which are as yet unforeseeable. Enlarging NATO launches us all on a voyage of discovery. Not only will it change NATO, it will also deeply change the environment in which NATO operates. It is therefore not surprising that opinions on enlargement are so divergent and intense.

Enlarging NATO will be an act of major political significance—not only for those who join, but also for those left out and indeed for those who are already Alliance members. That is why the study launched by NATO Foreign Ministers in December 1994 on the "how" of enlargement is so important. We need to prepare such a decision as carefully as we can. The NATO Brussels Summit of January 1994 accepted in principle that NATO would enlarge, although it did not specify the steps to be followed. Some analysts believed that NATO enlargement should follow in the wake of the European Union (EU)'s own enlargement, sometime in the early years of the next century. Others thought that too close a link between the two enlargement processes would not be advisable, but that an extensive period of preparation through the Partnership for Peace (PFP) program should precede NATO's enlargement. Still others hoped that an improving security situation and the development of good cooperative ties with Russia might obviate over time the urgency and possibly the very need for Alliance enlargement.

The undertaking of a study—which started immediately after the December 1994 ministerial meeting and has covered much ground since then—should not be seen as a delaying mechanism. Rather, it represents the first essential step in the process of enlargement—namely, the building of consensus among the existing 16 Allies on how new members will be brought into the Alliance. Unless all 16 Allies can harmonize their ideas and agree on the "how," there is no possibility of agreeing on the "who" and the "when."

From Rome 1991 to Brussels 1994

There will be no difficulty in "selling" membership of NATO to countries in Central and Eastern Europe. They have been clamoring for it since the Soviet Union and the Warsaw Pact disintegrated several years ago. But we may have more difficulties in persuading our own publics and parliamentarians to ratify enlargement, especially if the costs are not known and the additional security benefits it will bring are not clearly presented. This task should not be underestimated. Here the experience of the Maastricht Treaty ratification is salutary. It took almost three years for that treaty to be ratified, and in some countries the debate was so difficult and divisive that the EU's standing was severely damaged. We do not want to repeat that experience with NATO enlargement. It is, by the way, one of the big advantages of the internal enlargement study that the 16 governments will have a common, agreed "set of arguments" at their disposal in the forthcoming ratification debate.

The basic question to be addressed is whether NATO will remain an effective security actor after enlargement? In arguing that inclusion in NATO will give a necessary stimulus to the new democracies in their reform processes, we should not overlook what NATO has achieved during the years of the Cold War and its aftermath. It created the conditions for unprecedented security cooperation in a continent which for centuries preferred to achieve security through uncertain and unstable balances of power. Nor could the post-Cold War era of cooperation have been realized without NATO.

It is important to understand that NATO does not have to "go East or die"; it does not need to enlarge to remain relevant. Rather, the Alliance's relevance comes from the major role it has assumed in shaping European security. We are, along with other European institutions and countries, trying to construct a framework for European security that at once reduces the possibility of major conflict and, just as importantly, multiplies the opportunities for real security cooperation between countries. To put it another way, we are enlarging the benefits of the kind of close security cooperation that has developed over more than four decades among present Alliance members. One way of extending this relevance is to enlarge NATO's membership, but only if it is consistent with the new framework of European security.

In developing this framework NATO itself has undergone a profound and rapid adaptation to the new post-Cold War environment. After the November 1991 Rome Summit, NATO Secretary General Manfred Wörner concluded that NATO had become a new Alliance:

> The decisions taken at the recent summit of the North Atlantic Alliance in Rome signifies nothing less than the birth of a new Atlantic Alliance—an Alliance with a broadened political role, a new strategic concept, ever closer cooperative relations with the countries of Central and Eastern Europe, a stronger European pillar within the Alliance, and a new structure of forces which are considerably reduced. The Alliance reacted thus to the changed situation and by doing so once again proved its vitality.

The Rome Summit set the stage for a number of subsequent decisions. One of these was taken a scant month later in December 1991, when the North Atlantic Council (NAC) established the North Atlantic Cooperation Council (NACC) as a forum for discussion and concrete cooperation in the area of security and security-related issues. The purpose of the NACC was the projection of political stability which was (and continues to be) a fragile commodity in post-Cold War Eastern Europe. With the NACC came the beginning of NATO's outreach policy to its east. That was in late 1991. Two years later a substantial new addition was made in the form of the Alliance's Partnership for Peace (PFP).

The Brussels Summit in January 1994 that launched Partnership for Peace also decided that NATO would enlarge to admit new members. It is important to examine the inter-relationship of these two decisions. They both went far beyond the mere process of adapting NATO to the new international strategic environment. Both will be elements of the very foundations of the future European security architecture.

Some commentators have recently suggested that the Partnership had been oversold, that it lacked enough substance to provide the closer ties to NATO sought by many Central and East European states. But PFP has yet to achieve its full potential, and this cannot occur overnight.

The objectives of the Partnership are to:

- bring the new democracies of Central and Eastern Europe, as well as other Organization of Security and Cooperation in Europe (OSCE) member states, closer to NATO as a community of nations sharing the values of democracy, liberty, pluralism, and the rule of law;

- provide all partners with a means to develop ever closer cooperative military relations with the Alliance and other partners;

- develop transparency in defensee planning and budgetary processes, and thus enhance confidence among participating states;

- strengthen democratic control of armed forces; and,

- increase the capability and the readiness of states to contribute with NATO and other partner countries in the areas of peace-keeping, humanitarian aid, search and rescue, and other agreed activities.

If anything, the Partnership has been undersold. Its substance will accrue to NATO as and when the Individual Partner Programs (IPP) take root and depending on their nature. And that will be, as usual, a matter of initiative and resources which the Partners themselves bring to their programs.

Could enlargement damage PFP? By taking out presumably the most active present PFP participants, by discouraging those who do not join in the first wave, by developing a relationship with Russia beyond PFP; there may be a few countries tempted to reconsider the usefulness of their participation in the elaborate framework we have put in place. Enlargement may mean that we will have to find new ideas of substance to invigorate PFP to ensure that those outside the expanded NATO have an interest in further maintaining their cooperative ties with us.

This may particularly be the case with Russia. Russia remains the strongest military power in Europe, the only country that can change the political configuration in Europe through military means. For this reason, NATO allies have an enormous interest in helping the process of Russian reform succeed. If Russia develops along the lines of a market-oriented democracy, most of the pressing security problems in and beyond Europe would appear to be manageable, be they nuclear proliferation, regional conflicts, or conventional arms sales. By contrast, if Russia slides back into a confrontational pattern, crisis management in and beyond Europe would become far more difficult, to say the least. Would we have to resurrect a policy of containment as a result?

Of course, few people—either in the West or in Russia—believe that the current phase of domestic turmoil in Russia will end anytime soon. But this does not change the need to engage Russia in a constructive, open-minded dialogue on security matters of common concern. We could easily become victims of a self-fulfilling prophecy if we simply assumed that Russia was fundamentally un-reformable.

This is why an enhanced relationship with Russia must be part and parcel of NATO's enlargement process, and why this process itself must remain highly transparent. We are willing to take into account Russia's weight in European security and its legitimate security interests. In addition to the invitation to Russia to join the Partnership for Peace, we have offered Russia an enhanced dialogue and cooperation in areas where Russia and the Alliance have important contributions to make. It is unfortunate that Russia, after drafting the relevant documents together with us, then decided not to sign them.

More and more the message from Russia seems to be that Russia wants to make the NATO-Russia relationship a hostage to the enlargement issue. Russia interprets NATO's enlargement in outdated terms as part of "zero sum game." NATO members see enlargement as a step that increases stability and security in the whole of Europe and will thus be clearly also in Russia's interest.

The question becomes one of assessing the mood and prevailing political currents in Moscow, as next year's presidential elections draw nearer. How far does Russia want to take its relationship with NATO? Is it using the enlargement issue as a bargaining chip to obtain a more substantive consultative relationship—perhaps in treaty form—with NATO on the bigger political and security issues in Europe? I believe that the NATO Ministerial meeting at the end of May will address these questions, in assessing how NATO's cooperative relationship with Russia, both through PFP and beyond it, will impinge on the enlargement process and vice-versa. In any event, the last word on this matter has not been spoken. NATO and Russia are simply too important for European security to "artificially" ignore each other. Russia is too big to be isolated from Europe; it can therefore only isolate itself.

Specific Questions Regarding NATO's Enlargement

Since its inception, NATO has taken in new members on three occasions: in 1952 Greece and Turkey joined; in 1955, the Federal Republic of Germany; and in 1982, Spain. No enlargement studies were deemed necessary on these previous occasions. This reflects the fact that the enlargement being conceptualized and prepared today is categorically different from previous enlargements in at least three important aspects.

In the past, only particular countries were invited to join. Today the number of countries which might be invited amounts to no less than 10. On the personal, but probably plausible, assumption that NATO would not consider including CIS member-countries (i.e., Belarus and Ukraine—leaving aside here the very special case of Russia), options exist, at least theoretically, for the four so-called Visegrad countries (Poland, the Czech Republic, Slovakia, and Hungary), the three Baltic States (Lithuania, Latvia, and Estonia) and the three South-Central European countries (Romania, Bulgaria, and Albania). This means that the whole region of Central Europe, ranging from the Baltic to the Black Sea, is a possible subject for consideration. It is certainly true that some of these countries may have better chances than others, and some may have no realistic chance at all to be included in the foreseeable future. However, experience advises strongly against making any predictions.

Previous enlargements served primarily the purpose of extending protection to new members via the Article 5 guarantees of the Washington Treaty. However, the second main purpose of inclusion in the Alliance—that of integrating new democracies into the community of states sharing the same values—also played an important role in each previous enlargement. This was especially true in the case of Germany and Spain. It is reflective of the changed security equation in Europe that the main reason advanced by the Central and Eastern European countries for their wish to join NATO is not of a military, but of a political nature. They want to belong to the Western family of nations. NATO is considered to be the organization to join in order to belong to that community. This political rationale is certainly backed up and supported—in each individual case to various degrees—by perceived security concerns.

The relationship between political and security-related motives has, however, undoubtedly changed in favor of the political ones. This corresponds to the principal position of NATO that NATO's forthcoming enlargement must not draw new dividing lines in Europe, which means that it is not directed against any state. The practical implementation of this principle—that is the concrete modalities of the inclusion of new members in the political and particularly the military structures of the Alliance—will, in my view, be of crucial importance for our future relations with Russia.

Third, all previous enlargements took place within the framework of a rigorously defined European security structure and further cemented it. The forthcoming enlargement, regardless of whoever will be invited and whenever the invitation(s) will be issued, will be one pivotal element of an ongoing process of building a new security structure. This structure would center around an enlarged NATO linked with partners through PFP. It was from this perspective that U.S. Assistant Secretary of State Richard Holbrooke characterized the present juncture as "the fourth architectural moment"—following 1815, 1919, and the late 1940s, which were also times when Europe's basic security architecture was substantially reshaped into a relatively long-lasting, stable, and peaceful order.

Given the qualitatively different nature of the impending enlargement, the question also becomes one of where NATO must not change and how to ensure that it does not. If NATO's enlargement is to strengthen the security of the whole of Europe, including, of course, of its own member states, it must not lead to NATO's dilution. There is not a single decision which is not taken by consensus—the only conceivable rule for an organization charged with preserving the very security of its member states.

Reaching consensus among 16 sovereign states has never been an easy task. As Uwe Nerlich has observed: "The typical state of the Alliance was [one] of crisis over some kind of project that served as a vehicle for marginal repositioning within the Alliance, if not for domestic needs." Even so, the process of consensus-building in the Alliance, which has developed over more than 40 years of common work, is part of a unique political culture. Any new member state will need some time to adapt to becoming a fully fledged member, just as the Alliance itself will need time to absorb any new member. And, if anything, the cohesion and solidarity in decision-making will be more difficult than before, for the simple reason that pressure from an outside threat is simply not there in the same way as during the Cold War.

There is certainly no law of nature that determines that the process of consensus building, which works at 16, is doomed to fail at 16 plus X. It is, however, not unreasonable to assume that there is a limit to the size of the organization, beyond which the process of consensus-building would become just unmanageable. This might seem to be a rather abstract and theoretical argument, and to a degree it certainly is. It is, however, driven by an appreciation of the overall political situation in Central and Eastern Europe, and the network of inter-regional relations—and tensions—that exist. It is a region which is still—or again—fraught with unresolved ethnic and border problems, many of which are rooted in the peace treaties of Versailles, Trianon, and Saint Germain. It is possible that bilateral issues still not peacefully settled could come up anew, putting an additional burden on NATO's internal cohesion should these same countries be accepted as full NATO members. The export of stability by enlargement will unavoidably mean a certain import of instability.

This, of course, is not a totally new challenge to NATO. NATO was never only about collective defense against an external aggressor, but always fulfilled at the same time "collective security tasks"; the most striking example being, of course, the Greek-Turkish relationship. The fact that the fundamental security question—the question of "Peace or War"—is no longer a serious question, even not a question at all, among NATO member states is an achievement of NATO. It is only too obvious that some of the Central and Eastern European countries applying for membership wish to join in order to reap the benefits of this "collective security" function of the Alliance as a forum for peacefully settling bilateral problems. This is a perfectly legitimate motive and even welcome from NATO's point of view.

But when considering enlargement, the assets and liabilities that each state brings will have to be weighed very carefully in every individual case. There are clear limits which exist, beyond which NATO's structures, at least as they are now, would be overburdened and the consensus-building and subsequent decision-making processes seriously impaired.

The same line of reasoning also applies not only to relations between new members themselves and new members and individual current member-states, but also to relations between the new members and those left outside. The December 1994 NAC communiqué stated that enlargement must strengthen security and stability as a whole and should not draw new dividing lines. This means that new members must be prepared to support NATO's policies, including the provision of aid for those remaining outside the Alliance; NATO's dialogue and cooperation with Russia; and NATO's contribution to UN and OSCE peacekeeping missions. It also means that new members must actively reach out across their own borders to those left outside. It will be vital to ensure that new members, who join the Alliance and therefore assume all the obligations and rights which membership entails, do not block the accession of further states on selfish grounds. For all these questions there is no guarantee and no watertight solution. One can only hope that the collective political judgment and wisdom of the 16 or, at a later stage, possibly the 16+, will turn out to be right.

All this might sound somewhat paternalistic towards potential new members. But these are important points and we have to get them right. NATO's credibility and effectiveness, and to a certain degree its very essence, is at stake. It would be too high a price to pay if enlargement leads to the dilution of the Alliance as a "hard" security agency—to its degradation into a "weak" collective security institution with a large and disparate membership.

What political changes will be required after enlargement? And what will be the impact of enlargement on NATO's agenda? It is certainly fair to assume that common positions of NATO encompassing 16+X countries will differ from those of the current NATO at 16. As new members will be expected to accept the political "*acquis communautaire*," medium- and long-term issues on NATO's agenda—on which NATO's position is still evolving—are of particular relevance in this regard. It is clear that much will depend on the timing, the concrete modalities, and the scope NATO's enlargement process will take. What is possible at this stage is therefore no definite answers, but rather "educated guesses" and sometimes not even that. It might therefore be better to just ask the questions without giving an answer.

The most fundamental task NATO is facing for the years to come is certainly that of forging a new transatlantic bargain—to put our transatlantic relationship on a new foundation by fleshing out the twin pillar concept of NATO. Since 1994 NATO has made some headway in this concept with the proposal for Combined Joint Task Forces (CJTF). The new NATO-Western European Union (WEU) relationship, which is evolving, must in the longer run be followed by an equally coherent relationship between NATO and the European Union with whom the Alliance shares common strategic interests. What will be the contributions of new members to this debate, given that they seek to join the European Union and the WEU as full members as soon as possible and yet are very much dependent in defense terms on the transatlantic pillar?

Another long-term issue that comes to mind is the recent effort of NATO to project stability to its south, the Mediterranean initiative. Although five allies are situated along the Mediterranean, the overwhelming focus on east-west relations during the Cold War tempted the Alliance to overlook NATO's Mediterranean dimension. The recent Mediterranean initiative tried to re-create a balance between the east-west and north-south dimension. Should one assume that enlargement will more or less automatically re-direct NATO's focus on east-west issues at the expense of the southern dimension?

Another issue will be put on NATO's agenda by the very process of enlargement. How will NATO organize its relations with those Central and East European countries (except Russia) which will for whatever reasons not be invited to join the Alliance in the first wave?

Enlargement of NATO is not a political goal *per se*, but part and parcel of the process of building a comprehensive European security architecture, including the process of (re-)structuring the entire region of Central and Eastern Europe. If the inclusion of some countries in the Alliance will be perceived by those not invited to join as exclusion, leaving them in a "grey zone," a "no-man's land" of security, the consequences could be serious, leading to a decrease of stability rather than its increase.

Any enlargement of NATO must therefore be complemented by most determined efforts of the Alliance and bilateral efforts of its member states to draw closer to the Alliance those countries left out. An enlarged Alliance will have to *produce*—not only to seek, but to achieve in reality—a close cooperative relationship with those countries. The instruments for doing so are already available: the North Atlantic Cooperation Council provides those countries with access to the political consultative and decision-making bodies of the Alliance. PFP provides them with a flexible instrument for ever closer military cooperation; and in addition offers them the possibility of consultations with NATO in case of a direct and imminent military threat to their territorial integrity and independence. Our aim must be to make the difference between "export of stability" via inclusion in the Alliance and the "projection of stability" via PFP and NACC as small as possible. I mentioned already the possible need to re-invigorate PFP in order to keep it attractive for those countries which will not be included in the first wave and may have no realistic prospects to be invited in the foreseeable future. NACC, being basically confined to political consultations, and thus "weaker" than PFP—which focuses on concrete military cooperation—might be an even more serious problem in this regard.

Finally, there is the possibility of unwelcome political developments in Central and Eastern Europe induced by the very process of enlargement itself. Interlocutors from Central and Eastern European countries often make the point that the inclusion of their neighbor(s) without inviting also their own country, or at least giving it a concrete perspective to be also included at a later stage, would run the risk of creating serious internal problems and even political instabilities.

This should not be dismissed too early as being only part of a game of repositioning among potential new members. It makes it clear that it is necessary to "compensate" those countries left out in parallel to the process of integrating the new member states. The political and resource problems which NATO will face in order to successfully meet this challenge should not be underestimated. It is clear that new member-states will have a particular responsibility and vocation in this regard and will be expected to make some considerable contributions to this long-term undertaking which one can expect to put considerable additional strain on NATO's resources.

In summary, the hard decision to enlarge, will pose to NATO a broad range of difficult political and internal problems. It is my view, paradoxically, that this very fact might indicate that the decision to enlarge will, from a historical perspective, prove to have been the right one.

DR. CATHERINE McARDLE KELLEHER

Dr. Kelleher is the Defense Advisor to the U.S. Ambassador to the North Atlantic Treaty Organization. Before assuming her current position, she was a Senior Fellow in the Foreign Policy Studies Program at the Brookings Institution. Dr. Kelleher served as a staff member of the National Security Council during the Carter Administration, and was Professor in the School of Public Affairs at the University of Maryland. She has also taught at the Universities of Denver, Michigan, and Columbia, and was Professor of Military Strategy at the National War College. She has served as Director of the Center for International Security Studies, was a research fellow at the International Institute for Strategic Studies in London, and a visiting fellow at All Souls, Oxford. Dr. Kelleher recently completed a monograph entitled *The Future of European Security: An Interim Assessment*, outlining the changing nature of European security in the post Cold War world. She received her undergraduate training at Mount Holyoke College, her doctorate in Political Science from the Massachusetts Institute of Technology, and a D.Litt. from Mount Holyoke College.

The Military Dimension
11

Catherine McArdle Kelleher

The development of thought on the precise military implications of NATO enlargement is really still in its beginning stages. There are studies being conducted in Washington, in Brussels, and at the RAND Corporation (by Richard Kugler, see Chapter 12). We are at the point of consideration, but not yet at the point at which any decisions are being made or requirements established.

Indeed the process of carrying out the enlargement study within the Alliance has been an attempt to determine what the Alliance itself sees as the parameters that will be set for new members to consider as they make application to join the Alliance.

As in all NATO decisions, the final arrangements will depend on the choices of the member states and the needs and decisions of the Alliance itself. And even though we are looking perhaps at a broader enlargement than we have before, we are still looking at the same process, namely case-by-case, state-by-state, mindful of the particular legislative and cultural traditions of those members in terms of the military policies and postures of the Alliance.

Assumptions For the Military Implications of Enlargement

The first assumption I should make is that much of what this chapter addresses cannot be talked about until the Alliance itself has decided on the "who" and the "when" of enlargement. At the moment that is not a subject being discussed within the Alliance. However, it has added much to the grist of op-ed writers in the United States and great speculation in a number of capitals. A set of assumptions guide the study at NATO and will continue to guide the discussions, particularly on military implications. Perhaps the principal assumption, on which there is no debate, is that if a state joins NATO, it has all of the rights and all of the obligations of a full Alliance member. There will be no second class members of the Alliance.

NATO is still a military as well as a political alliance. The critical difference between participation in the Partnership For Peace (PFP) program and membership in the Alliance is that a "member" becomes a full participant to the degree that it chooses to do so and the Alliance chooses to accept those conditions in the Alliance's military posture. That means first and foremost that all of the rights and obligations involved in the Article 5 guarantee apply. More importantly, it also means the rights and obligations that are assumed under Article 4. Alliance members have a commitment to consult, and to be heard; a right to raise issues of national security with other Alliance members; and they may form coalitions of the willing to deal with the defense of Alliance interests outside of the narrow borders of Alliance territory.

Another set of assumptions are embodied in the Strategic Concept, enunciated formally in November of 1991. It remains the overall guidance for the military structures and decisions that will arise out of enlargement. First, it says that the new risks are different, in both quantity and quality, from those faced by the Alliance in the past. At the core are the expectations that under present international conditions, conventional military forces are considerably more involved, and that the Alliance will deal at most with the unlikely possibility of a near term, untoward reversion in the East to the prospect of a massive invasion of Europe. What is expected is a set of conflicts which might entail minor regional contingencies at most, as well as questions of proliferation, terrorism, or conflict arising out of ethnic tensions. Thus, these are the new risks Alliance security, those arising out of conflicts that happen elsewhere.

Last but not least, another assumption is that NATO defines itself as having no adversary, and of constituting no adversary to any state. There was a very different planning assumption in the old days, one which required a very different kind of exercise than the one that we must master now. Even the vocabulary that we've developed over the four decades of Alliance cooperation is not sufficient to the kinds of tasks we face. But the Alliance has already begun the process of transformation and what we see now with enlargement is simply an extension of that process.

Dimensions of Transformation: Force Dispersion, Force Differentiation, and Force Coordination

Implementing Alliance strategy in an enlarged NATO raises three issues. First, the **dispersion of forces** will have to change. Specifically, the question is often raised about the stationing of foreign forces on the territory of new members; this is a question that has been answered in different ways throughout the Alliance's history with respect to the wishes of particular member states. As members join, they assume the right and the obligation to contribute their own forces for Article 5 purposes. As with current members, their choices with respect to peacetime deployment and stationing will be those agreeable to both national authorities and the Alliance as a whole. Certainly these will be matters for consideration beforenew states enter the Alliance. But, there can be no doubt that in times of crisis and war, the Alliance must retain the possibility of transit and stationing on the territory of any new member. Otherwise, the Article 5 guarantee makes little sense.

The second issue is **force differentiation**. Studies within the Alliance over the last several years have stressed that NATO is moving towards smaller, active duty forces, this will be clearly a consideration for a number of states, old and new members, that have not had a tradition of professional forces in the past. The smaller active duty forces can be deployed as multinational rapid reaction forces reinforced by mobilizable reserves. These forces, defined by the Rome and subsequent decisions, will be able to deal with minor regional contingencies as they arrive. They will certainly be able to take the kind of timely action necessary to confine crisis and conflict. This will put a different kind of requirement on all the members of the Alliance, including new members, in terms of the mobilization of reserves. They will have to plan seriously about the kinds of capabilities that can be mobilized over a long period of warning without disruption to their economic and democratic structures.

The third issue is the **coordination of forces**, which is perhaps the central element in the change of the existing military force structure. From the perspective of the United States, the integrated military structure is the *sine qua non* for military effectiveness. One challenge facing NATO is how to continue the process of adaptation of headquarters and command structures that has already taken place over the last three years. But one needs now to re-examine the question of the location of headquarters and the need to develop greater regional bonds, among both the existing and new members. Given the challenges of enlargement, the Allianace may well have to simplify further the command structure, perhaps with the absence in some cases of a formal echelon of command. It could be replaced within NATO by some derivitive of the Combined Joint Task Force (CJTF) concept, as a way to organize forces to ensure military effectiveness in specific areas.

With respect to **nuclear doctrine and posture**, the Alliance should keep the formulation of "nuclear weapons as the last resort," meaning a weapon which is available to the Alliance and which must be planned for. But, at the moment and under existing conditions, no one sees a need for change in either doctrine or posture to accommodate new requirements posed by the conceivable range of enlargement scenarios.

However, the Alliance will need **new, combined capabilities**, ones that encompass a number of new areas of emphasis and interests. We should include here the efforts being made to secure common funding for ground surveillance capabilities and theater ballistic missile defense. NATO, as a whole, should take both challenges far more seriously than present discussions within the Alliance may sometime suggest.

Instruments of Transformation

Independent of the precise new members and their particular military needs, we have at hand a number of the instruments which allow this vision of the future to happen. The **CJTF concept**—long in the coming, and to be decided this year—surely is an instrument which, if used correctly, gives us far greater flexibility and far more of the kind of organizational military effectiveness we will need against an uncertain threat. Within PFP, we now have the **Planning and Review Process** (PARP) with 14 Partners. It is a modified version of the Defense Planning Questionnaire (DPQ) process to review national forces that are available for the three PFP missions—peacekeeping, search and rescue, and humanitarian assistance. This is a process of creating not only transparency but also dialogue and a degree of parallel or convergent evolution in defense planning that will stand us in good stead as we face the question of military change.

In bilateral channels, particularly for the United States, there are also a number of other initiatives. First is the path-breaking effort, already in place, to match American national guard and reserve units on a state-by-state basis with Partner nations. This will help develop understanding of the reserve concept and foster a kind of civilian responsiveness, expanding the German concept of the citizen in uniform or the American idea of the citizen-soldier in new ways. Second, there is the proposal, made under the President's Warsaw Initiative, for a joint air traffic control management system that has now been expanded to include most of the states of Central and Eastern Europe. This initiative involves low tech solutions to a common problem and will allow for joint management most of the European air space.

For both of these projects, the key for our Partners is the same: namely, interoperability. This is a goal which, to some degree is still to be achieved with NATO, despite four decades of rhetoric. But for new and old members, this objective is essential to ensure that enlargement represents a new gain in overall security.

But the most important instrument of all is a well known military doctrine: *no surprises*. This means transparency in decisions, transparency about expectations, and transparency in the kind of joint planning and preparation that we do in the future. This process will take longer than enlargement proponents, who see this simply as a political problem, wish to believe. It will, however, take less time than many of those who are critical of NATO enlargement would like it to take.

NATO, particularly in the military sphere, is a way of doing business. It is a way of doing business that has evolved and changed considerably over the last six years. It is a way of doing business that has always appealed to national interests and calculations of effectiveness. More importantly, it has proven itself in a number of different environments and scenarios to be the most effective way of multiplying capabilities and minimizing risk.

Although the road is going to be long, and the task quite complex, we are well on the way to making the kinds of changes, and building the kinds of capabilities, that will be necessary to bring about an enlargement that strengthens the military as well as the political effectiveness of the Alliance. The goals first set in Washington in 1949 continue to be as vibrant and as relevant as before: cooperation in assuring the security of those governments that share the ideals of the Atlantic Charter and that support the peaceful extension of democracy's fruits to all interested states.

DR. RICHARD L. KUGLER

Dr. Kugler is currently Senior Social Scientist and Associate Director International Security and Defense Policy Center, RAND. Other assignments at RAND include Associate Head, Political Science Department, Santa Monica, California from 1988 to 1990 and from 1990 to 1991 he was Senior Social Scientist in Washington. Dr. Kugler served as Director, Strategic Concepts Development Center, National Defense University from 1984 to 1988. From 1980 to 1984, Dr. Kugler was Director, European Forces Division, Office of the Secretary of Defense for Program Analysis and Evaluation, and from 1975 to 1980 he was assigned as Senior Analyst in the Asia and European Division. Dr. Kugler's academic career includes Adjunct Professor of International Relations, George Washington University from 1979 to 1988 and Faculty Member, RAND Graduate School from 1988 to 1991. His publications include two books, three major RAND reports, seven scholarly articles and forty DoD studies, all on NATO/European security affairs and U.S. defense policy. He earned a Ph.D. from the Massachusetts Institute of Technology and a B.A. in Political Science from the University of Minnesota.

Defense Program Requirements
3

Richard L. Kugler

Although the task assigned to this chapter is that of addressing the "Infrastructure Question" arising from NATO enlargement, the challenge facing the alliance will go far beyond that of merely creating an appropriate military infrastructure, as this term is commonly defined. When NATO analysts speak of "infrastructure," they normally are referring to the nuts and bolts of what underlies a force posture. This includes road and rail systems, reception facilities, ammunition storage sites, POL pipelines, ports, airbases, interoperable weapons, common training, and the like. To be sure, a host of important infrastructure issues will rise to the fore as enlargement occurs.

But military infrastructure will be only one part of a much larger challenge facing the alliance. The larger challenge will be the fashioning of an overall "defense program" so that appropriate security arrangements vis-a-vis new members can be brought to life. In addition to infrastructure, this program will need to include initiatives for creating a command structure, and for upgrading the forces of new members while making them operationally compatible with NATO's forces. It also will require measures for improving the capacity of current NATO forces to work with the forces of new members, to help defend their territory, and to carry out other security missions with them. Only when this larger defense program is developed will it be possible to determine infrastructure goals and the host of other measures to be pursued.

Accordingly, this chapter focuses on the larger "Defense Program Question." It seeks to shed some speculative insights on the looming issue of:

- What kind of coordinated defense program will NATO and its new members need to adopt as enlargement occurs?
- How can this program best be carried out, how much will it likely cost, and who should pay for it?

In grappling with these tough questions, this chapter's purpose is not advocacy; nor does it pretend to offer definitive judgments about either programs or costs. The analysis of this entire topic is only in its infancy: a great deal of planning and analysis must be accomplished before anything concrete can be known. This effort merely endeavors to illuminate the issues and alternatives that may lie ahead, and to offer a general sense of the magnitude of the challenge facing NATO. Its purpose is to help educate and inform, not to prescribe anything specific.

In order to focus the analysis, this paper assumes that the four Visegrad states—Poland, the Czech Republic, Hungary, and Slovakia—will be joining NATO by the end of the 1990's. No claim is made here that the future is destined to unfold precisely this way. NATO has not yet fashioned a schedule for enlargement. When it does so, NATO may choose to admit only one or two countries by the turn of the century, and more than four in the aftermath. Consequently this assumption says nothing definitive about how enlargement will begin or end. What it provides is merely a convenient mechanism for crudely gauging the programmatic agenda ahead. By allowing us to form an estimate of what may be needed to incorporate the four Visegrad states, it provides a reasonable basis for making inferences about the enlargement process in general, regardless of which country is admitted and when. All of the accompanying data, especially budget costs and force levels, are illustrative and unofficial. Official data will be available only after NATO, SHAPE, and the participating countries have had an opportunity to study these issues in far more depth than can be provided here.

The Need For A Strategic Perspective

The best place to begin this analysis is to put things in proper perspective, for before the trees can be studied, the forest must be seen. The current debate on NATO enlargement is largely cast in political terms. Defense issues typically are deemed secondary or too hot to handle. Yet postponing the inevitable is not normally a good idea—especially when important matters will soon be at stake.

The act of admitting new members is truly a strategic undertaking, one that must be guided by a coherent sense of Alliance policy and strategy. During the Cold War, NATO was preoccupied with deterrence and defense to the point where its activities took on a largely military character. Happily, those dark days have passed into history. The primary purpose of NATO expansion into East Central Europe (ECE) is not to erect a Western military bloc there or to wage a new Cold War, but rather to help pursue larger political and economic objectives. These goals include strengthening democracy, bringing the ECE states into the Western community, keeping European Union (EU) and NATO membership in rough tandem, and fostering peaceful integration across Europe. At its heart, nonetheless, NATO remains a collective defense alliance. Wherever it goes, a security agenda of some sort will follow in its wake. This has always been the case in the past, and it will remain true as NATO enters the ECE region in the coming years.

The idea of keeping new members at arm's-length distance from NATO's defense mechanisms may appeal to some. So may the parallel idea of creating a kind of neutral zone in East Central Europe where the alliance's political commitments are made, but organized coalition defense activities do not take place. The viability of both ideas falls apart when the Alliance's essence is considered. When they join, new members will become permanent parts of the NATO family and household, not mere neighbors.

The act of expanding NATO will create two-way commitments and involvements that go far beyond those fashioned by the North Atlantic Cooperation Council (NACC) or the Partnership for Peace (PFP). NACC and PFP are important vehicles for establishing a security dialogue with former Warsaw Pact adversaries, and for creating a climate of growing cooperation. By contrast, formal entrance into NATO is a far more serious endeavor for everybody. New members will be required to accept all of the duties and responsibilities that accompany Alliance membership. NATO, in turn, will accept a solemn treaty obligation under Article 5 to help give these countries a sense of security and protect them from external aggression. The result will be a tight bonding of these countries to the entire alliance. Today these countries are new friends with which the alliance is becoming familiar, but to whom it has no deep commitments. Once they join, these countries will become strategic blood brothers of NATO's current members. The Alliance will be obligated to help protect them through thick and thin—in peace, crisis, and war.

The strategic importance of this Article 5 commitment is magnified because all of these new members reside in a region that is legendary for its chronic volatility. Some years ago, the alliance welcomed Spain into the fold. This step was troublesome enough, but it was eased because Spain was not directly threatened by anybody. The act of admitting new members from East Central Europe will be a somewhat different proposition. Fortunately, Europe no longer faces a hegemonical threat akin to the Cold War. Indeed, there are reasonable grounds for hope that Russia will emerge as a market democracy and a close partner of the West. Even so, nobody can be certain of what the future holds. This is the case for reasons that go well beyond worry about Russia.

The entire ECE region, as well as the Balkans and Eurasia, are laced with many historical rivalries, simmering ethnic feuds, uncertain borders, and other geopolitical fault-lines. Perhaps these troubles will fade as market democracy and Western institutions spread across the region. Yet they remain realities today. The desire to gain protection from them is a primary reason why the Visegrad Four want to join NATO. In important ways, these countries will be entering NATO as "front-line states": as countries that, while not exposed to a direct military threat, are situated on the frontier of the new era's emerging geopolitics.

To cite the Article 5 commitment is not to deny that it will play a vastly different and less center-stage role than was the case during the Cold War. Then, fear of a major war was an ever-present reality. Article 5 consequently was at the forefront of NATO's *raison d'etre*. In the coming years, the atmosphere will be more peaceful across all of Europe. Article 5 will take on the status of a backup reserve clause: a valued insurance policy, but one unlikely to be called upon. Moreover, the defense contingencies to be worried about will be far less threatening than during the Cold War. Then, theater-wide conventional war and even nuclear conflict animated defense planning. In the coming era, defense planning will focus on a spectrum of less threatening contingencies, most of them at the low end of the spectrum of violence.

Even so, the underlying if easily overlooked reality needs to be kept firmly in mind when the future defense agenda is contemplated. Enlargement is more than just a political act. It is also a security and military step. NATO and ECE forces will be drawing close to each other for strategic reasons that go beyond learning how to operate together, or conducting purely peacetime missions, or promoting the larger cause of political integration. They also will be learning how to wage war together, and how to carry out collective defense commitments that will remain one important part of NATO's mission in life.

The security and defense requirements of these new members thus are something to be taken seriously by NATO as a whole. These countries will enter the Alliance as nations perceiving a need for military protection from a host of contingencies: some big, others small; some imagined, and others real. The Alliance will be legally obliged to work with them to craft this protection even as it takes parallel steps in diplomacy and economics to render the entire continent peaceful and democratic. Because the future is so uncertain, the worst thing that could be done is to extend a hollow political commitment whereby these countries are allowed to enter the alliance, but appropriate steps are not taken to fashion the security guarantees needed to help meet their defense requirements. In this event, these countries will have gained little by joining NATO. Equally important, NATO will have acquired entangling new commitments in a potentially dangerous region, but it may lack the capacity to carry them out at the moment of truth. To avoid this disastrous outcome, enlargement will need to be accompanied by appropriate defense arrangements required to bring the Article 5 commitment and related security missions to life. This is the beginning point for putting enlargement into proper strategic perspective.

The solemnness of this Article 5 commitment does not mean that NATO faces the task of fostering a level of military preparedness anywhere near to that of the Cold War. Indeed, the opposite will be the case. The dangers, threats, and requirements of the coming era will be far less than during the troubled past. For this reason, NATO's defense preparations can be commensurately smaller. In all likelihood, there will be no need for a major and outwardly provocative NATO military presence in East Central Europe in peacetime. Barring the unexpected, new members can be protected by improving their own forces, and by configuring NATO's forces so that modest numbers of them can move eastward in the event of a crisis. Consequently, the defense agenda ahead likely will not be an imposing one. It will not necessitate an earth-shaking upheaval in NATO's defense plans, forces, strategy, and budgets. The alliance has undertaken far more demanding tasks many times in the past, and successfully carried them out. NATO therefore can approach this agenda with a calm sense of confidence that its resources will not be overwhelmed, and that the steps needed to defend new members will not themselves provoke a new Cold War with Russia.

Nonetheless, the alliance should not underestimate the complexity and demanding nature of what lies in store. Although this agenda will be manageable, it is not something that can be dismissed as trivial, or as easily accomplished in the absence of concerted effort. Defending new members will require the performance of military missions that go well beyond PFP, which focuses mostly on peacekeeping and similarly modest operations. More will be involved than merely making ECE forces "interoperable" with NATO forces in a purely technical sense. Forces from new members and current NATO countries will need to be welded together so that they can carry out true coalition operations of a fairly demanding nature.

Acting together, these forces will need to become capable of fulfilling new Article 5 commitments and carrying out other NATO military missions, such as peace-enforcement and crisis interventions outside the ECE region. At the moment, they are not fully capable of doing so. The problem lies partly with ECE forces and partly with NATO's own forces, both of which reflect their Cold War heritages. The act of bringing these forces into the new era and joining them together may be no more formidable than what NATO has experienced in the past, but it will be demanding enough in its own right. This agenda is not one that NATO can afford to ignore, or shrug off as too simple to worry about. The alliance will have to pull up its socks and get to work.

Exactly what will NATO need to do? In a nutshell, it evidently will need to fashion a comprehensive defense program of some sort to accompany enlargement. The term "defense program" means a coordinated set of measures aimed at creating the military capabilities needed to carry out specific missions and attain well-defined security objectives. It can be large or small, but it normally is characterized by the blending together of numerous separate but interrelated activities over a period of time, often several years. Regardless of its size and character, what marks it is the expenditure of money, resources, and energy on behalf of a concrete purpose. It can involve the creation of something entirely new out of wholecloth, but equally often, it necessitates merely a limited set of improvements needed to bridge a partial gap between an existing military capability and a perceived requirement. Happily, this latter state of affairs will be the case for NATO when enlargement occurs.

The ECE and NATO combat forces needed for the new missions and objectives already exist, as do most of the support assets. Thus, an expensive enlargement of the Alliance's military posture will not be necessary. What seemingly will be needed is a far less expensive set of programmatic measures aimed to reconfigure existing forces so that they can operate effectively together, perform the new coalition missions assigned them, deal with the contingencies of the future, and thereby render NATO's new members as secure as the rest of the Alliance. Even so, these measures are nothing to be sneezed at. What is involved here is the combined defense of a new region well outside NATO's current borders and its old Cold War military perimeter, in interaction with national forces that, as of today, are not designed to operate with NATO's forces. The gap between existing capabilities and future requirements is not overwhelming, but when the thorny details are considered, it seems significant. This gap is eminently bridgeable with a patient effort over a period of time. Yet bridging it will require NATO and its new members to expend some energy on behalf of a common purpose. A remedial and constructive defense program will be needed—not sometime in the distant and discountable future, but fairly soon, for the future is arriving with a rush.

Budget Costs And Force Goals

How much will the entire enterprise cost? This question is hard to answer with any single, fixed estimate. The reason is that the cost will be a variable, not a constant. It will depend upon the force goals and military horizons that NATO sets for itself, and upon the programmatic measures to be pursued, which can be few or many. An organizing concept will be needed, and NATO can turn to its own history for a variety of models. During the Cold War, military exigency compelled it to defend AFCENT with a large, multinational joint posture deployed near the old intra-German border. Yet NATO protected the flank countries through different models embodying alternative combinations of self-defense, logistic support, air forces, and ground forces through power projection. All of these models, and new models besides, will be available to NATO as it decides how new members are to be made secure.

If the Alliance's goal is merely to configure ECE forces to defend themselves with NATO help only in the areas of C^3I and logistics support, then the cost will be relatively low. If the alliance decides to supplement this commitment with sizable NATO combat forces through a purely power-projection strategy from Western Europe, the cost will rise. The cost will grow further if steps are taken to develop a military infrastructure in East Central Europe so that NATO combat forces can deploy there quickly. Depending upon the choices made in these areas, a reasonable estimate is that the alliance-wide, 10-year "out of pocket" cost for a satisfactory program probably will fall in the range of $10-50 billion. Along with these direct costs, there likely will be a need for a security assistance program to the ECE states in the form of Foreign Military Sales (FMS) loans and grants to help finance replacement of obsolescent weapons.

As will be discussed below, this $10-50 billion is the expense deriving from NATO enlargement over-and-above the spending already programmed or otherwise required to maintain ECE and NATO forces at currently planned preparedness. It is the additional amount needed to bring NATO security guarantees and treaty commitments to life by upgrading ECE and NATO forces in the required ways. Up to $20 billion reflects the cost of preparing ECE forces and infrastructure for NATO membership and missions. The remainder is the cost of configuring NATO forces for projection missions and equipping them with a forward infrastructure so that they can deploy rapidly to the east. This estimate, it is noteworthy, assumes that NATO refrains from stationing large forces in East Central Europe and that improvements to the ECE infrastructure are relatively austere. If either of these assumptions are violated in major ways, the cost could rise far higher—up to $100 billion or more.

If a cost of $10-50 billion is an accurate estimate, this is a plausibly affordable amount. By comparison, the life-cycle cost of a U.S. Army division is about $60 billion, and the acquisition cost of individual U.S. weapon systems often runs $20-30 billion or more. Yet in today's climate of fiscal stringency, it is not a trivial amount. Moreover, the difference between the low- and high-ends of this estimate is large. The low-end buys one kind of capability; the high-end, something better, but more expensive. Where along this continuum does NATO want to fall? How much defense preparedness in East Central Europe does the alliance want, and how much is it willing to pay?

The program question boils down to the old hardy perennial that has confronted NATO since its inception: "How much is enough?" Because no single theory of military requirements stands out as the obvious choice, a strategic judgment will have to be made. NATO will need to make judgments about the level of insurance to be sought, the degree of risk to be accepted, and the theoretical dangers to be hedged against in an era of political ambiguity. The Alliance will need to decide upon the nature of the security relationship to be crafted with the new ECE members, and upon the military strategy to be pursued. Once again, the Alliance will be confronted by the necessity for choice, and by the need to balance impulses that pull in opposite directions. The manner in which NATO chooses to balance these countervailing impulses will determine the costs of enlargement. The Alliance will have a variety of options at its disposal, with ascending levels of military commitment and capability. In the final analysis, policy and strategy will be the key driver of the choice.

Powerful factors will argue in favor of a modest program solely focused on making the ECE states militarily self-sufficient, and therefore not undertaking any special steps to prepare NATO combat forces to participate in their defense. These factors include the scarcity of defense funds across NATO, competing modernization priorities, the belief among some that the ECE region will be stable in absence of any weighty military shadow cast by NATO, and reluctance to do anything provocative that might upset Russia.

The drawbacks of this limited approach, however, are obvious. The ECE states that will be joining NATO are all small or medium-sized powers. They will have military establishments capable of handling minor emergencies, but not fully capable of defending their borders and vital interests against larger regional dangers. All of these countries will be looking to NATO to provide not only moral support and logistics help, but also reassurance that sufficient Alliance combat forces will be available to help them in a dire emergency. As full-fledged members of NATO, these countries will have legal rights to assurances of adequate protection: rights that are as powerful as those belonging to the Alliance's oldest members. To the extent that these assurances are not provided, the vitality of NATO's collective defense pledge will be eroded. What good is an expanded but diluted Alliance? If some members are defended less effectively than others, is not the entire collective defense pledge eroded?

For its part, NATO will have powerful incentives to back up its collective defense guarantees with combat forces of some magnitude. After all, the best way to exert influence over a fluid strategic situation in peace, crisis, and war is to provide combat forces, not merely logistics support. But what kind of combat forces, and in what quantities, will be enough? Will tactical air forces alone suffice? If so, how many fighter wings will be needed? Will ground forces also be required? If a joint posture is required, will a small force suffice: for example, 3 divisions and 5 fighter wings? Or will a much larger force be needed: for example, 10 divisions and 10 fighter wings? And what should be the internal mix of the posture selected? Should it be composed of air intercept forces and lightly configured ground units, or should it involve multimission air units and heavily armored ground forces?

The answers to these questions are anything but obvious, and will be determined by the strategic, political, and military goals that NATO sets for itself. What can be said is that the answers embraced by NATO will have a major impact on determining the budget costs of expansion. Because NATO's force posture today is not well-configured for projection operations into the ECE region and major missions there, each additional increment of combat power can be purchased only at a price. If NATO is satisfied with the capacity to project rather small forces in a slow-paced fashion, the cost may be minor. But if the goal is to project fairly large forces rapidly and effectively, the cost will rise. In all likelihood, NATO will not be able to afford, much less need, the permanent stationing of large combat forces in the ECE region in peacetime. Yet even a largely power-projection strategy from Western Europe will not be a free lunch, for significant programmatic measures will be needed for this strategy to be brought to life. Budgetary restraints may argue in favor of limited efforts, but military prudence may pull in the opposite direction.

If the budget cost for the entire program proves to fall near the high-end of the spectrum, its relative importance and cost needs to be kept in strategic perspective. The ECE states will be required to carry their fair share of the load, but they will lack the resources needed to upgrade their own postures and infrastructure to meet NATO standards, much less pay for a power-projection strategy from Western Europe. NATO's current members therefore will be required to carry a large share of the financial burden.

Claims that a sizable program is unaffordable are belied by the fact that it will amount to only about 2-3 percent of what NATO already plans to spend in defense of current borders that are no longer seriously threatened. Even recognizing that small changes in spending patterns can have an upsetting effect, can room not be found for new programs to defend the part of Europe and NATO that genuinely may be endangered? Again, the answer may not be easily arrived at, but as enlargement unfolds, NATO may find itself coming face-to-face with the question.

This expense, moreover, should not be seen exclusively through the prism of NATO enlargement. Many of the measures contained in a sufficiently robust program might well be needed even if NATO does not enlarge. If enlargement does not occur, after all, the goal of defending the ECE region will not go away. Indeed, it might be harder and more expensive to accomplish if the ECE states are kept out of the Alliance, for the benefits of coalition planning will be lost. In addition, the act of configuring ECE and NATO forces in these ways will provide strategic benefits that go beyond merely protecting East Central Europe, for these forces will be better able to project power and operate together elsewhere. Within the ECE region, the effect will be to make the prospect of expensive crises and wars far less likely. These strategic considerations make the budget costs of NATO enlargement more bearable.

Regardless of how the costs are appraised, the key point is that NATO has multiple options at its disposal. It is not imprisoned by history, its present force posture, a menacing enemy, overburdening military requirements, or by inflexible budgetary realities. The Alliance can carry out the military dimensions of enlargement in a variety of ways, with costs that range from truly small to fairly large. Moreover, it can navigate the future with a step-by-step approach that surveys the situation at each stage, and adjusts its defense efforts accordingly.

Yet the Alliance does need to begin planning and deciding, for when strategic priorities are at stake, muddling through is almost always a bad idea. Equally important, NATO must begin thinking about these matters fairly soon. NATO treaty commitments will apply on the day new members join the Alliance, not several years later. Because the lead time between program inception and execution is fairly long, the Alliance will need to know how it plans to defend its new members at the time when they join the fold. Indeed, NATO would be best advised to get a jump on the process by beginning now, for momentum will soon start building, and it should be guided in the right direction.

What NATO needs to do is to bring its well-oiled force planning process to bear. Focusing on the coming ECE defense agenda, it needs to craft a strategic concept, a military strategy, balanced force goals, and appropriate programs that are adequately funded. A top-down approach of this sort is needed to avoid the fallacy of acting on multiple different fronts without a guiding vision in ways that are almost destined to produce a poorly construed outcome. Even with a sound approach, the act of preparing ECE and NATO defense arrangements for the coming era is not one that can be accomplished overnight. What likely will be needed is a

10-year plan; one that establishes coherent goals, coordinated programs, cost-control standards, and fair burden-sharing practices.

A plan of this sort would amount to something conceptually similar to NATO initiatives of the past: Allied Defense In the 70s (AD-70), the Long Term Defense Plan (LDTP), and Conventional Defense Improvements (CDI). A ten-year plan would not accomplish everything. The full process of integrating ECE forces and defense plans into NATO will take considerably longer. But the essential foundations can be laid over the course of a decade. A carefully managed, slow but steady ramp upward seems better than either perpetual delay or a mad rush to achieve everything at once. This gradual, but visionary approach has worked for NATO before, and provided it begins fairly soon, it can work again. The key lies in NATO getting its strategic bearings straight from the onset.

Preparing ECE Forces And Defenses

Any effort to contemplate the manner in which the ECE defense establishments should change in order to prepare for NATO membership must begin by recognizing the disadvantageous historical legacy inherited by them. Until only a few years ago, all of these countries were decades-long members of the Warsaw Pact. Their defense postures were designed to support a coalition military strategy, crafted by the USSR, which aimed at posing an offensive threat to Western Europe and NATO. Each of their postures played a specialized role in this Warsaw Pact strategy. They were designed accordingly. Their command structures, doctrine, tactics, and procedures reflected the Soviet model. Their ground and air forces—both combat units and logistic support assets—mimicked the Soviet approach. Virtually all of their weapon systems were either manufactured in the USSR, or at least designed there.

This historical legacy is important because the old Soviet/Warsaw Pact model is so vastly different from the NATO model in many critical respects. The most obvious difference lies in basic military strategy. Whereas the Warsaw Pact strategy was offensive, NATO's strategy is defensive. Underlying this difference are major dissimilarities in the very fundamentals of military philosophy—differences that reflect not only the distinction between totalitarian and democratic values, but also dissimilar geostrategic situations, economic systems, and historical experiences at waging war. The Soviet/Warsaw Pact model reflected an emphasis on ground operations, quantity, combat formations, firepower, simple technology, and regimentation. By contrast, the NATO model emphasizes the opposite: joint air-ground operations, quality, a mix of combat forces and logistic support, maneuver, high technology, and individual initiative. These major differences penetrated to the depths of the force postures on both sides. Warsaw Pact C^3I structures, combat forces, and logistics units were arrayed very differently from those of NATO. Their training patterns, readiness standards, weapon systems, maintenance practices, and support systems were equally dissimilar. Everything taken into account, it is hard to imagine two military alliances so radically different in their approaches to coalition operations and warfare.

Owing to this historical legacy, the magnitude of the challenge facing the ECE states is very great. For the past five years, these countries have been pursuing the goal of building downsized national defense establishments aimed at protecting their individual borders. They have made considerable progress at casting off the past, but they still have a long distance to go. As they enter NATO, they will face an entirely new requirement: that of adopting the ways of a new alliance, with a very different approach to military affairs. In essence, the ECE defense establishments will face the formidable task of embarking upon a second revolutionary upheaval at a time when the first upheaval is not yet complete. The extent of the transformation facing them upon joining NATO is great, and it will be complicated by the act of entering an alliance system as integrated and pervasive as that of NATO. This transformation will not be completed in the course of only a few years. Yet over the course of the coming decade, it can be initiated in important ways.

As the ECE states enter NATO, they will be primarily responsible for maintaining the size, readiness, and modernization of their own forces. Although all are downsizing their forces from old Cold War levels, their national economic problems and dwindled defense budgets limit the financial resources available for military spending on the roughly 20 mobilizable divisions, 1000 combat aircraft, and other forces that will remain. As of today, most apparently are spending about 3-4 percent of GNP on defense, and their GNP's are not large. If their economies recover under the stimulus of market capitalism and Western investments, additional resources may become available for defense. Barring an economic miracle, however, the likelihood is for a slow, but steady increase—not a major upsurge.

From the amount of money available, the ECE defense ministries will face the problems not only of maintaining fairly large postures at adequate readiness, but also of modernizing forces whose weapons will become increasingly obsolescent in the coming years. The inventories of the ECE states reflect varying age profiles, but on whole, their weapons are mostly based on technology from the 1970's or earlier. Most weapons can be kept in service for many years with adequate maintenance and periodic upgrades, but at some juncture all have to be replaced. Even if a normal rate of turnover occurs, roughly 25-50 percent of their major weapon systems will face replacement over the next decade. Although the ECE states produce some weapons and support vehicles on their home soil, they will need to acquire a fair amount of equipment from abroad. This especially is the case for modern combat aircraft, which will dominate the cost of their modernization programs.

Because the ECE states now operate Soviet-style equipment, continuity would argue in favor of buying replacement models from Russia, which is now launching an effort to rebuild its international weapon sales program. The need to build ECE force postures along NATO lines, however, argues in favor of buying Western models from the United States, Germany, Britain, France, and other manufacturers. The drawback is that Western equipment tends to be expensive owing to its sophisticated technology, modern munitions, and demanding maintenance and training requirements. The financial squeeze can be lessened by buying at the low end of the technology scale, and where possible, procuring rebuilt models rather than new weapons hot off the production line. For example, a used but rebuilt F-16 can cost much less than a newly minted, advanced version.

Even so, the ECE states likely will require Western security assistance in the form of loans and grants in order to modernize at a sufficient pace. The amount of assistance needed is uncertain and will depend upon a variety of factors, but a reasonable estimate is roughly $1-2 billion annually. This security assistance will have less of an impact on Western defense spending than new acquisition programs that must be funded directly out-of-pocket. Yet, it will have a major impact in influencing the degree to which ECE defense establishments are able to draw close to the NATO model. If these countries are compelled to keep old Soviet-style weapons or to buy new Russian-built models, they will remain somewhat outside NATO's military orbit irrespective of steps to promote commonality elsewhere. But if they steadily acquire Western aircraft, tanks, and infantry fighting vehicles, they will come to look and act like NATO for this reason alone. Moreover, the transition will be rendered far easier in many other areas, including interoperability, training practices, and common military doctrine.

Along with this normal modernization will come a need for a host of other, less visible programmatic measures that are required to interlock ECE forces with those of NATO, to enhance their self-defense capabilities, to build a better military infrastructure, and to help meet treaty commitments once membership is granted. All of these measures will need to be funded out-of-pocket, and most are over-and-above current defense plans. Many will have to be funded by the ECE states. But a number can qualify for NATO security investment (infrastructure) funds. Still others may be partly funded by individual NATO countries that see advantages flowing to their own growing defense commitments in the ECE region. As discussed earlier, the ten-year cost of a relatively austere set of measures is likely to be $10-20 billion taking into account acquisition and operations costs. If the investment faucets are opened more fully, the cost could rise higher, but the need to control expenses seems likely to beget a modest approach.

One of the important issues affecting not only the new members but NATO as a whole will be that of creating a command structure to supervise defense activities in the ECE region. The complexities of this subject go far beyond this chapter's scope. Suffice to say that NATO civilian and military authorities doubtless will study the issues and alternatives thoroughly. The basics deserve mention, however, because they will influence the costs of the defense program and the way that the entire enterprise is carried out. The idea that the ECE states might remain outside NATO's integrated command—like France—appeals to some for political reasons. But powerful military incentives may arise for new members to join in order to gain the full strategic benefits of NATO membership and to help empower the Alliance to carry out its commitments to them. The real issue, therefore, may not be whether they join the integrated command, but the extent to which they become integrated within NATO and with each other.

A variety of models are available, ranging from deep integration to a relatively mild outcome. The deepest model is that of AFCENT during the Cold War. The severe threat to Central Europe compelled NATO to form a highly integrated multinational command composed of two Army Groups and two numbered Air Forces, which commanded the forces of eight nations. These forces operated quite closely together, and had a war broken out, they would have fought side-by-side in a layer cake array.

The post-Cold War era has seen the old forward defense scheme go away, but integration has deepened in AFCENT owing to creation of multinational corps. In the northern and southern regions, by contrast, a looser form prevails. This owes to geographic realities, political factors, and a lesser threat during the Cold War. Although NATO multinational reinforcements were planned for each country during the Cold War, defense planning was conducted mostly on a national basis, but under supervision of regional NATO commands: AFNORTH (now AFNW) and AFSOUTH. Although the tradeoffs will need to be weighed closely, the strategic situation in the ECE region may lead to adoption of some version of this second model. That is, the forces of the ECE states may draw close to NATO, but air defense aside, they will not necessarily be joined with each other to form a single, unified defense posture.

Even so, some type of regional command structure may be needed, as continues to be the case in the northern and southern regions. Recently, NATO adopted the idea of Combined Joint Task Forces (CJTF's), and plausibly this solution could be applied. Task forces, however, are best-suited for single operations, not guiding complex defense preparations over a period of years. This argues for something similar to AFSOUTH. Perhaps AFCENT might be extended eastward, or an AFEAST created, or a subsidiary body established. Regardless, some command facilities probably will need to be built. The program requirement could include a central structure, principal subordinate posts, an intelligence center, and communication linkages to national defense ministries and assigned forces. This structure could be mildly expensive if existing facilities are deemed inadequate.

Far more expensive could be the task of configuring ECE forces to become at least minimally compatible with NATO forces and standards. In particular, ECE air defenses seemingly will require a major and potentially expensive face-lift. Apparently a new medium-to-high altitude SAM system should be installed, along with improved radars and communications nets. Fighter interceptors will need to be rewired for NATO munitions and safety standards. For both combat aircraft and ground weapons, technical compatibility will need to be fashioned through a host of measures: common fuels, munitions, nozzles, radio frequencies, and the like. The readiness of several air and ground units may need to be enhanced. NATO training practices and safety standards will have to be adopted. An intensified exercise program with NATO could be needed to help promote common doctrine and procedures. ECE military personnel will need to attend NATO schools in large numbers. All of these changes cannot be achieved overnight, but even a step-by-step program could prove fairly demanding of resources.

Measures to improve the ECE military infrastructure also could prove fairly widespread and therefore expensive. Owing to the Cold War and their membership in the Warsaw Pact, all of the ECE states have rather elaborate military infrastructures. But in some places, these infrastructures evidently are eroded, or poorly configured for the new era, or inadequate for NATO's requirements. Steps to improve them might include upgrades to road and rail systems, Polish ports, POL production and distribution systems, telecommunications systems, airbases, ground installations, and exercise facilities. Also important, measures might have to be pursued to reconfigure and enhance ECE war reserve munitions and stocks. This could produce expensive acquisitions of ammunition, spare parts, replacement end items, better maintenance equipment, and storage facilities. The total volume could be high. Some of these changes will take place owing to the natural evolution of ECE economies and defense programs, but as these countries join NATO, pressures likely will arise to accelerate the improvements.

The exact cost of all the programmatic improvements to ECE defense establishments will be known only when comprehensive plans are formed. What stands out from this cursory review is the sheer number of separate endeavors to be launched, and the magnitude of the potential requirements owing to the admission of possibly four new members. Measures in Poland likely will be the most demanding, but requirements in the other three countries could add up to a sizable whole. An improved air defense system alone is likely to cost several billion dollars. A new NATO command structure, other upgrades to ECE forces, infrastructure enhancements, and acquisition of war reserves could further increase the total by a significant amount. For these reasons, a total cost of $10-20 billion seems plausible even if the fiscal faucets are not turned wide-open. Yet this expense is hardly staggering when seen in relation to the costs of maintaining NATO as a whole. Even today, after 45 years of building the

Alliance, NATO's annual infrastructure budget alone is about $875 million—or nearly $10 billion for ten years.

The need to fashion a program to align the ECE defense establishments with NATO is apparent. Yet, the challenge should be kept in perspective lest it become a basis for paralysis. The dominant factor in the equation is that the new members already possess well-armed military postures, and are capable of carrying their fair share of the load. Thus, NATO does not face the task of protecting the unprepared or unwilling. The ECE postures will need to be reshaped to reflect the NATO model, but there is no pressing urgency for them to adopt all of NATO's multitudinous practices and procedures immediately. What the situation requires is sufficient military compatibility to carry out common defense missions, not carbon-copy postures. This raw-bones compatibility is achievable in fairly short order. Once it is attained, the task of refining the details can be pursued in a step-by-step fashion over a period of years. Picture-perfect standardization and gleaming infrastructures are desirable goals, but in the final analysis, they are means to a strategic end: not ends in themselves. If they had been criteria for launching the Alliance enterprise, NATO never would have been formed in the first place.

Preparing NATO Forces For New Treaty Commitments

NATO will have little difficulty providing C^3I and logistics support to new members, but to the extent that NATO must back up its treaty commitments with combat forces, it will have a constraining historical legacy of its own to overcome. The Cold War left NATO with a powerful posture for defending Alliance borders, but not well-designed for power projection outward. The United States has long thought in projection terms, and it has become fairly good at the enterprise. But apart from maintaining a capability for projecting small forces for minor incidents, most West European countries still have military establishments mostly designed for border defense. If new treaty commitments are to be carried out in the ECE region but large forward deployments there are ruled out, this legacy will need to be overcome, for NATO will have to become skilled at a projection strategy.

To be sure, the act of defending East Central Europe will be far easier than protecting the distant Persian Gulf. Yet, the distances in Europe are not inconsequential. The eastern borders of Poland and Hungary are located fully 1,000 kilometers from NATO's bases and logistic facilities in Western Germany. This distance lies at the outer limits of airpower's reach, and is beyond the reach of ground forces without a major redeployment. Europe's impressive rail system will ease the task of eastward deployment in a crisis.

But a major constraining factor enters the equation here. The Persian Gulf deployment was possible because the U.S. military came equipped with a large theater logistics structure capable of supporting West European units. The defense of East Central Europe will be conducted more heavily by the West Europeans, with U.S. forces playing a less central role. As of today, most West European forces—including German forces—do not possess the deployment, mobile logistics, transportation, and service support assets to fully carry out this mission. As a result, they too will need to change. Some of the changes already are underway, but the process has only just begun. It will need to be accelerated as NATO enlargement draws near.

The act of choosing the source of NATO forces to help protect new members will be an important one. Surface appearances might suggest that NATO's Rapid Reaction Force is the obvious candidate. But it will be needed for other missions (e.g., defense of Turkey), it is designed for corps-sized missions at most, and it is heavily populated by lightly-equipped ground units and forces from Southern Region nations. A better candidate may be AFCENT's Main Defense Force. Yet, it is especially wedded to its Cold War logistics base, it lacks large mobile support assets at echelons above corps, and its multinational formations may further complicate the act of rapid projection. If it is to help defend the ECE region, it may have to undergo important changes to its composition by acquiring a far better capacity for outward deployment eastward. This especially will be the case if requirements turn out to be fairly large, not small. In any event, strategic realities dictate that commitments primarily should come from NATO's major powers: the United States, Germany, and Britain. Modest forces from the Low Countries, through multinational corps, would broaden the political base. Participation by France also would be a good idea.

The cheapest and easiest solution would be for NATO to provide only tactical air forces. The rationale for this approach presumably would be a "division of labor" philosophy whereby the ECE states would handle ground missions for which they have large forces, and NATO would provide help in areas in which it enjoys a relative advantage. As discussed earlier, however, powerful strategic and military incentives may lead to the commitment of NATO ground forces in one quantity or another. To the extent this is the case, the cost will rise, for the act of configuring a single West European division for projection can cost over a billion dollars. If the required joint posture turns out to be small (e.g., 3 divisions and 5 fighter wings), the cost will be fairly small. But if the requirement becomes large (e.g., 10 divisions and 10 wings), the cost could rise much higher.

Another important factor will be the extent to which a military infrastructure is developed in East Central Europe to enhance the prompt deployment and effectiveness of NATO combat forces. For example, NATO might decide to deploy POMCUS sets and WRM stocks onto the soil of new members. It might also establish COBs airbases, ground reception facilities, and training sites there. It might further decide to base small combat forces there (e.g., 2-3 brigades and air wings) to provide a signal of reassurance and better combined training opportunities. Depending upon its size, a military infrastructure of this sort could be fairly expensive.

What could truly drive the cost sky-high is a decision to permanently station large combat forces in the ECE region: for example, corps-sized forces or more. This step would entail the creation of a quite large support infrastructure: command staffs, large service support units, and facilities for civilian dependents. However, budgetary constraints, to say nothing of strategic impediments, make this step improbable as long as East Central Europe remains a tranquil place.

Short of this unlikely step, a modest military infrastructure aimed at supporting a power-projection strategy would be less expensive, but not inconsequential. The cost of this infrastructure would be added atop the expense of configuring NATO combat forces for projection missions. The overall expense would be determined by the ambitiousness of NATO's force goals in both areas. It could range from a few billion dollars to upwards of $30 billion for a ten-division, ten-wing posture with a fairly substantial forward infrastructure. When combined with the cost of preparing ECE forces and infrastructure, the total bill could rise from $10-20 billion to about $50 billion. This amount, however, is an outer limit. The cost could be less if NATO's force goals and programs turn out to be more modest. A reasonable best guess is a ten-year cost of about $35 billion for a controlled upgrading of ECE defenses and a modestly sized NATO military commitment.

Once again, this cost needs to be kept in strategic perspective. The cost is no larger than that of acquiring a single, active duty ground combat division, and not much larger than that of buying a single modern weapon system in large quantities. The strategic gains are quite large, for a program of this magnitude will transform a potentially hollow commitment into something credible. Regardless of how the tradeoffs are appraised, the key point is that the cost will be driven by policy and strategy—not by unavoidable fixed expenses over which NATO has no control. NATO can spend as much, or as little, as it wants to spend. Everything depends upon the goals that NATO sets for itself, but the nature of these goals matters if the strategic purposes of expansion are to be achieved. The key lies in studying the issues thoroughly and then making a sound choice.

Burden-Sharing And Investment Strategy

Assuming the program cost is $35 billion, this amount may be small in the overall scheme of things, but when account is taken of competing priorities and tight limits on defense spending everywhere, it is not something to be taken lightly. All the more so since this program would require a major increase in NATO infrastructure funds, and either modest budget increases or program sacrifices elsewhere by participating nations. This amount of money will become available only if approval is granted by national leaders and parliaments. But the presence of politics means that the enterprise will be scrutinized carefully before it is launched. Who then pays? How are the financial burdens to be distributed?

Based on financial realities and traditional NATO practices, the ECE states probably can be expected to pay for about 20-30 percent of the total: the amount needed to fund national programs and their fair share of common infrastructure spending. The remainder presumably must come from NATO's current members. Two models are available for allocating the responsibility. The first model is one in which the countries participating most heavily with force commitments, and with the greatest interests at stake, provide the financing. In this case, a core group composed of the United States, Germany, and Britain (perhaps also France) would be obligated to provide not only most of the forces, but also 70-80 percent of the money. To the extent NATO's other powers enjoy the strategic benefits, they would get a free ride.

The second model is one in which the costs are shared by the entire Alliance even as a smaller subset handles the key force commitments. In this event, the financial burden carried by the core group might decline, for example, from $27 billion to $16 billion. Of the two models, the second would do the best job of preserving coalition planning and fair burden-sharing. Yet history suggests that, in cases like this, something approximating the first model is the one often adopted.

Regardless of how the burdens are shared, the prospect of a ten-year plan means that an investment strategy should be forged for guiding the enterprise from start to finish. A variety of alternative strategies are available, and they should be weighed carefully. The traditional approach is to initiate all of the program sub-elements at the onset, and to fund them in parallel fashion as the enterprise unfolds. The advantage is that consensus is forged behind the entire program at the onset. The disadvantage is that, if funding falls short or the program is halted mid-stream for political reasons, an incoherent outcome may be the result because none of the sub-elements are completed.

An alternative strategy is a building-block approach whereby the key subcomponents are funded sequentially, in order of opportunity or greatest strategic leverage. For example, NATO might use the years preceding enlargement to upgrade its own forces for projection missions. New members thereby would enjoy a greater level of NATO protection on the day they join the Alliance. In the immediate aftermath, investments could focus on improving the self-defense capabilities of new members. At the end, emphasis could switch toward developing a forward infrastructure for NATO's forces. The advantage of this approach is that NATO could test the waters as it goes, gradually ascending from one strategic plateau to another, while postponing the most controversial decisions until the political situation in Europe is clarified. The disadvantage is that consensual support for the entire program might not exist from the onset, and this absence could impede execution when difficult items are encountered. The Alliance might end up with half a loaf.

Most likely, a mixed strategy will prove best. Historical experience suggests that coalition planning works best when consensus is formed behind a complete plan from the onset. Yet a comprehensive plan can be executed in flexible ways. The years prior to admission may provide an opportunity—one that should not be lost—for improving NATO's posture and starting to work with new members through security assistance. To the extent key goals are achieved, relative emphasis can then switch to improving the ECE postures and slowly building a NATO forward infrastructure to the extent that the political traffic will permit or demand. Regardless, the key point is that, while NATO enjoys flexibility in choosing how to proceed, it will need a coherent investment strategy to avoid the dangers of incoherently muddling along. The greatest danger lies in adopting no investment strategy at all.

In conclusion, although today's debate over NATO enlargement is cast largely in political terms, a defense agenda seems destined to rise to the fore sooner or later. The simple but powerful reason is that Article 5 commitments are involved, and the Alliance's military posture will need to be arrayed to carry them out. This chapter suggests that the coming defense agenda is manageable, but that NATO will soon need to begin thinking in terms of a long-range program. NATO's own experience shows that establishing a sensible destination and a strategic plan to get there is the best way to shape the future, and thereby avoid being victimized by it. If this analysis is broadly correct, the budget costs of preparing NATO's defenses for enlargement are not trivial, but they are affordable. To be sure, the act of pursuing the necessary military measures will not be a free lunch. But it will bring major strategic benefits in its wake, not only in East Central Europe but for NATO military missions elsewhere. Above all, it is the only way to avoid the worst of all possible worlds: a hollow NATO enlargement that leaves everybody no better off than before, and maybe worse for the wear.

*U.S. G.P.O.:1997-418-297:60009